# *Village* ~~Walks~~
## — in —
# WEST YORKSHIRE

## Richard Bell

COUNTRYSIDE BOOKS
NEWBURY, BERKSHIRE

COUNTRYSIDE BOOKS
3 Catherine Road
Newbury, Berkshire

ISBN 1 85306 541 2

Designed by Graham Whiteman
Photographs, maps and illustrations by the author
Front cover photo shows Bramham village

Produced through MRM Associates Ltd., Reading
Printed by Woolnough Bookbinding Ltd., Irthlingborough

# Contents

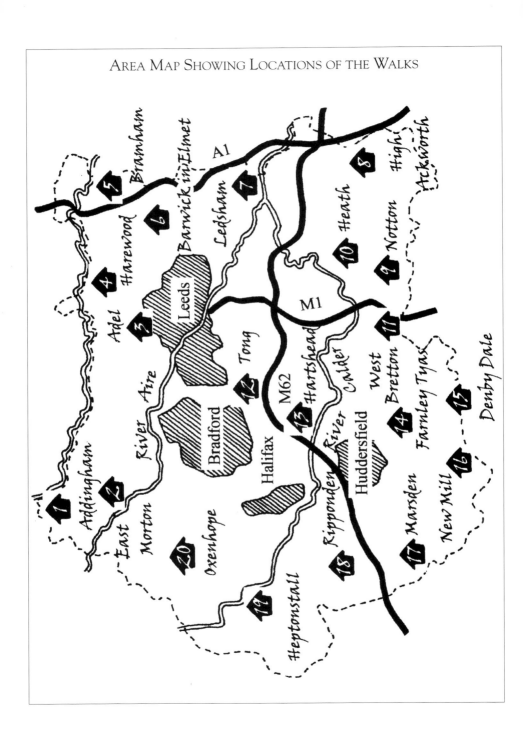

AREA MAP SHOWING LOCATIONS OF THE WALKS

## Publisher's Note

We hope that you obtain considerable enjoyment from this book; great care has been taken in its preparation. Although at the time of publication all routes followed public rights of way or permitted paths, diversion orders can be made and permissions withdrawn.

We cannot of course be held responsible for such diversion orders and any inaccuracies in the text which result from these or any other changes to the routes nor any damage which might result from walkers trespassing on private property. We are anxious though that all details covering the walks are kept up to date and would therefore welcome information from readers which would be relevant to future editions.

# Acknowledgements

My special thanks to Roger Gaynor, John and Heather Gardner, and Martin and Terry Housley who, between them, suggested seven of the 20 routes.

Where would we be without footpath officers? My thanks to the various officers with responsibility for footpaths in each of the five local authorities, who cast an eye over these routes and, in a handful of problem cases, advised on suitable alternatives. They include Stephen Jenkinson, Ray Morse (Bradford), Mr M.J. Overend (Calderdale), Mrs S. Dixon, Mr R. Malkin (Kirklees), Roger Brookes (Leeds), Mick Burkinshaw and Virginia Moulton (Wakefield).

Thanks also to Matthew Webster, Fiona Mitchell, Tim Melling (RSPB), Robin Horner (RSPB), Susan Parker, Trefor and Liz Higgs, Mr Wraith, Joan Smith, Christine Williams-Brown and members of my walks group (who tested some of the walks). Finally, special thanks are due to my wife Barbara who had to put up with me when routes that looked fine on the map ended up at a bridge that had rotted away or in a trench-like path neck-deep in nettles (don't worry, neither of those made it into the book!).

The books which I have consulted most frequently while compiling the walks have been Arthur Mee's *The King's England, West Riding* (1948 edn.), *The South and West Yorkshire Village Book*, compiled by members of the counties' Women's Institutes, and Leonard Markham's two books of *West Yorkshire Pub Walks*.

# Introduction

Visit the vineyard, stroll up to the hill village, explore the limestone gorge...yes, you're in West Yorkshire, at Swillington, Heptonstall and Wentbridge to be precise (see walks 7, 19 and 8). Put on your boots and discover bluebell woods, hay meadows, cloughs and moors around villages featured in film, novel and television comedy.

On a clear day, as you start back across the fields towards Ledsham from Fairburn village, you can see Holme Moss television mast on the crest of the Pennines above Holmfirth, 28 miles away. You're looking right across the length of West Yorkshire, from North Yorkshire to Cheshire. In one sweep you can see the three main landscapes that make up the county: the bare gritstone moors, the limestone ridge on which you are standing and, between them, the gentler hills and valleys of the Yorkshire coalfield.

The busy A1 behind you is just the latest ridgeway route to follow the magnesian limestone scarp. The Romans came this way, as did William the Conqueror. Many of the footpaths that you'll follow in these walks date back almost as far. There are packhorse trails, lanes used by cattle drovers, railway walks and canal towpaths. Reminders of the Industrial Revolution include weavers' cottages on the edge of the sheep moors and, down in the valley, the gritstone mills that grew up to replace them.

I hope you enjoy exploring West Yorkshire as much as I did when preparing these walks. I've lived here all my life but I found lots of places tucked away that I'd never visited. For instance, I'd often passed through Denby Dale, the Pie Village, but never found the intriguing little 18th-century settlement hidden away nearby at Quaker Bottom. I've whizzed past Hartshead services on the M62 without realising that there are sweeping views across open countryside around the village itself on the higher ground above. The walk around Hartshead takes you within bow-shot of the place where Robin Hood (a Yorkshireman) died. The Luddites used to meet at a local landmark called the dumb steeple and Charlotte Brontë was a pupil, and, later, a teacher, at a nearby school.

I couldn't resist including a walk at Oxenhope that takes you to the Brontë Parsonage itself, passing through scenes celebrated in the film of E. Nesbit's novel *The Railway Children*. Anyone who has seen *The Last of the Summer Wine* will find the South Pennine landscape on the New Mill walk (no 16) familiar.

But it's not just the film locations that are worth visiting; all the walks in this book have their individual charm. Images that come to mind include the wall of a Roman fort at Ilkley, views across the Vale of York to the white horse of Kilburn from Bramham, and a sign at one Pennine farmhouse: 'Never mind the dog – beware of the wife!'

If Yorkshire ever gets its independence the seat of government will have to be Castle Hill, a prominent landmark south of Huddersfield. Cartimandua, Queen of the Brigantes, is said to have held court here around AD 55. If she hadn't had a quarrel with her husband Venutius, which led to her calling in her allies the Romans,

Hadrian's Wall might have been built between the Humber and the Mersey and you might now be setting out to enjoy *Village Walks in the Kingdom of Brigantia*.

All the villages are easy to get to, most being within 10 miles of Leeds or Bradford. All of the walks are circular and can be completed in a morning or afternoon, but on the longer ones it is pleasant to take a lunch break and make a day of it. You won't starve on these walks; I've pointed out some of the tea shops and pubs, and the odd village shop. Looking at my reviews you might think that these walks were made in search of the perfect bacon sandwich, but, I can reassure you, the food on offer is far more varied. Car parking locations are indicated in the text – but if they are full, or for some reason unusable, please ensure that you park your vehicle in such a way as not to be a nuisance to those living close by.

Starting at Addingham and ending at Oxenhope, the walks are a clockwise tour of the county. A sketch map accompanies the description of each walk. For those requiring more detail, I have also given details of relevant Ordnance Survey sheets in the Explorer, Pathfinder or Outdoor Leisure (1:25 000) series, with a grid reference (GR) for the start of the walk. In the South Pennines, from walk 16 onwards, the slopes start to get steeper and the walking a little more challenging. Even so, most of the routes are still fairly level across the moors or along the gritstone edges and wooded valleys.

*Richard Bell*

# ADDINGHAM

*Length: 5 miles*

| **Getting there**: Follow the signs for Addingham village from the A65 Ilkley to Skipton road. Alternatively, start the walk at Ilkley which is accessible by rail. | **Parking**: There are two limited-stay car parks, one on the main street and one on Bolton Road. There are also a few parking spaces just off the road near the start of the walk. | **Map**: OS Explorer 27 Lower Wharfedale (GR 083499). |
|---|---|---|

The old stone cottages and weavers' workshops of Addingham sit with their backs to the river in a broad sweep of Wharfedale. Walking alongside the River Wharfe gives a quite different perspective to the one you get hurrying by in the car. The green fields, trees and woodland of the dale contrast beautifully with the bare gritstone edges of the moors above. The broad, U-shaped section of the valley was formed by an Ice Age glacier which gouged out the dale.

Surrounded as it is by sheep farms, it's not surprising that Addingham had strong links with the wool industry. There were once six mills here. The Rookery is a relic from that time, a stone-built double terrace originally operating as loom workshops

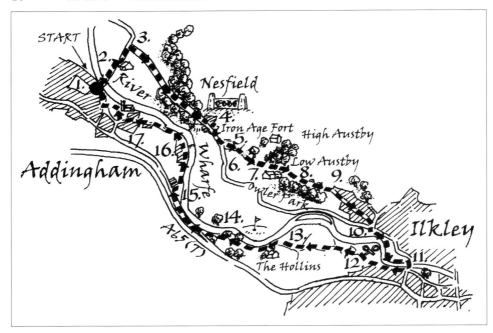

where 80 people lived and worked. You'll find it 200 yards up Bolton Road, near the school. Samuel Cunliffe Lister, a typical Victorian entrepreneur, is buried in the church. He made and lost fortunes, inventing wool-combing machines and a process for turning silk-waste into carpets and velvet.

According to ballad, in the time of Henry VIII local men left Addingham led by a 'Shepherd Lord' to fight in the Borders war. Perhaps they were present at the culmination of the conflict when the English defeated James IV and the Scots at the Battle of Flodden in 1513. Back in 876 the Archbishop of York fled here when the city was attacked by Vikings.

This walk takes you to Ilkley and back through water meadows and woods along quiet roads and riverside paths. There is an Iron Age fort, a packhorse bridge and, if you take a short detour into Ilkley, you can see part of the wall of a Roman fort which probably dates back to the 4th century, near the Manor House Art Gallery and Museum.

The walk starts at the end of North Street, Addingham, which you find by leaving the main street at the eastern end of the village and heading towards the river, not far from the church.

THE WALK
❶ Near the corner where North Street becomes Bark Lane, look for a cobbled footpath to Beamsley, opposite 5 Bark Lane, 'Four Gables'. Ignoring the Dales Way to the left, take the zigzag path down to the suspension bridge. Cross the bridge and follow the metalled footpath ahead for 250 yards.

right and about 30 yards from it.

---

**FOOD and DRINK**

If you're in Addingham on a weekend between mid-May and October try St Peter's church hall for afternoon teas and home-made cakes. It's pleasant to sit overlooking the green where Town Beck flows past the church and the groups of stone cottages. Otherwise, the ivy-clad Fleece on the main street looks worth trying. Telephone: 01943 830491. The main street also offers a Crown with pool, darts and dominoes, a Swan with a varied menu of lunches and evening meals, and a Sailor which has snacks, traditional lunches and evening meals with a beer garden at the rear. There are also two fish and chip shops, one with an attached restaurant.

---

❷ At the end of the path turn right across the brook, through a gate, then immediately left around the farm building, passing two horse chestnuts to reach the lane.

❸ Follow the lane up to a road junction, then turn right in the direction marked 'Nesfield ¼ Ilkley 3'. This lane takes mainly local traffic, but look out for cyclists.

❹ After 1 mile you pass Castleberg Iron Age fort, grassy earthworks in a field on your right. At the hamlet of Nesfield turn left up the track by some cottages to make a detour to see the little village green, with its stocks. Then turn right and follow the lane down the hill, to rejoin the road you were on.

❺ Turn left along this road, leaving the village, and after 100 yards, just after the road crosses a stream, look for a footpath signed to High Austby on the left. Take the stile between the two field gates. Don't take the track up the hill but head across the field, keeping parallel to the road on your

❻ After 50 yards, follow a wire fence and head for the stone step stile by the oak tree in the far right-hand corner of the field. Ilkley comes into view across Wharfedale. Follow the drystone wall on the right-hand side of the next field. Several large oaks, some three to four hundred years old, give the impression that this has been parkland.

❼ After a conifer plantation on the left, below High Austby Farm at the top of the slope, take the stile ahead by Low Austby Farm.

❽ Keep left of the gate and up-slope from the private lane to Low Austby Farm, to the left of the magnificent old oak ahead. As you approach the wood the path dips into a gully, which might be an old trackway. Cross a little bridge, then climb to a wooden stile to cross a wire fence. The path through the wood descends into a deeper dip.

Ignore a wooden gate on your right and cross a wooden stile, then turn right up a grassy slope. Continue onward up the slope, across the meadow, veering left away from the fence. Cross a little gully in the field by some stone setts. Take the stile ahead into Owler Park Wood.

Oak and ash with bluebell, enchanter's nightshade, dog's mercury, ramsons and ferns show that Owler Park is ancient woodland. It has been managed by selective thinning and some replanting to create glades and allow new growth.

❾ Leave the wood by a squeeze stile by Owler Park Lodge and turn right down

Owler Park Road. After ¼ mile, turn right to cross Nesfield Road.

⓾ Take the footpath to the left behind the electricity substation opposite. Follow it alongside the river for ¼ mile, then take the old stone bridge to cross the Wharfe.

⓫ On crossing the bridge, turn immediately right at the nursery. Turning left here would take you along the Ebor Way to York, (around 35 miles) but the riverside footpath is the first part of the Dales Way which ends at Lake Windermere (73 miles to Bowness).

Follow the path with the river on your right. Fifty yards from the bridge, at the end of the first block of flats and just before a drain grid, look for flood marks carved in the wall; '1965 December', is the highest, with '1875 AD' visible a little lower down.

⓬ Continue ahead along a short stretch of lane to Ilkley Tennis Club. By the clubhouse take the footpath signed 'Dales Way' on your left, through an iron kissing-gate.

Follow the footpath across the meadows and through every kissing-gate you come to. After ½ mile you follow a watercourse on your left, dotted with yellow monkey flower in the summer, back towards the river.

⓭ At the river follow the path to the left, over a footbridge and through a small wooded area called the Hollins. Hollins was the name given to an area of hollies which were cut to feed stock in mid-winter.

*Packhorse bridge over the Town Beck.*

Cross another footbridge, then climb a small slope to come out at a footpath which you follow to the right, back towards the river bank. You'll find giant bellflower, meadow cranesbill, knapweed, common valerian and meadowsweet flowering here in summer.

**⓮** Continue across the meadow area, crossing makeshift stepping stones by some white willows. Look out for dippers on this riffled stretch of the Wharfe.

On reaching the old A65 turn right and follow the road alongside the river. The new A65 trunk road is up on the embankment on your left.

**⓯** After ¼ mile take the right-hand turn along Old Lane to Smithy Greaves and Holme Ings, marked 'Dales Way' on a public footpath sign.

**⓰** At Addingham Low Mill follow the road through the village, which was restored from a group of old mill buildings in the 1980s.

---

**PLACES of INTEREST**

In Ilkley there's the **Manor House Art Gallery and Museum**. Telephone: 01943 600066. **Cow and Calf Rocks** above the town are decorated with elaborately carved Victorian graffiti which include quotes from the scriptures. Graffiti these days just isn't the same. In the other direction, about as far as Ilkley, there's **Bolton Abbey**, which has attractive woodland walks.

---

At the far end of the village take stone steps up to the river bank. Follow the river-bank lane past a terrace of whitewashed stone cottages.

**⓱** Passing the Rectory on your left and the grounds of the Old Rectory on your right, take the public footpath on your right. Go down some stone steps to cross the Town Beck by a packhorse bridge, to reach a village green near St Peter's church.

Follow the church drive back towards the village and take the footpath over another small packhorse bridge to return to North Street; then turn right to return to the starting point of the walk.

River Wharfe, Addingham
Low Mill

# EAST MORTON

*Length: 2¾ miles*

**Getting there**: East Morton lies just off the B6265 between Bingley and Keighley.

**Parking**: There is some on-road parking by the small park in the centre of the village, near the toilets and the Busfeild Arms. There is also space for one or two cars at the roadside at the start of the walk on Green End Lane, opposite the track to Moorlands Farm.

**Map**: OS Explorer 27 Lower Wharfedale (GR 101425).

East Morton is an attractive mix of stone built Victorian terraces interspersed with some sturdy 17th-century houses. It lies on the edge of wild open moors looking out over the broad expanse of Airedale. East and West Morton are mentioned in the Domesday Book but the area's history goes back much further. A brass chest, probably a military pay chest, found in 1775, contained nearly a hundredweight of Roman coins. Cup-marks, perhaps the oldest form of art, have been found on boulders near the village.

In Charlotte Brontë's novel, Jane Eyre is promised a post at 'the new school now being built at Morton'. This was the national school (1845), built at the request of the vicar to compete with the non-conformist school across the road (now the village institute). In one stone-floored classroom 76 girls and 76 boys were taught for a fee of 2d or 3d per child per week. The school ran into problems with accusations of financial irregularities, questions in Parliament and the suicide of the vicar. It was demolished in 1978, and the site is now the village green.

Morton once had its own bus company and vehicles that have served the village have included the 'Old Agony Wagon' and the 'Morton Flying Pig'. Passengers were asked to get out and walk across the stone canal bridge which features in this walk, a safety precaution that didn't cease, officially at least, until 1980.

East Morton lies on the edge of Rombald's Moor so you could hike from here to Ilkley; however, this short circular walk along farm tracks and towpaths stays in Airedale. Like Wharfedale, Airedale has the features of a glaciated valley. It is U-shaped in section, without the interlocking spurs of river-carved valleys such as that of the Calder at Hebden Bridge. Along this stretch the River Aire occupies a valley which it did little to shape.

The stretch of the towpath of the Leeds and Liverpool Canal is not a public right of way but British Waterways encourage its leisure use. Always take special care of children when visiting the waterways and towing paths, particularly near locks.

THE WALK

❶ Beyond the last houses on Green End Lane (which leads off the main street on the same side as the Busfeild Arms) take the track on your left and follow it to Moorlands Farm.

❷ The footpath goes behind the farm, with the buildings on the left-hand side. You will have to negotiate the sometimes muddy entrance to the farm used by the cattle, which takes you through two gates. Please leave the gates as you find them.

❸ Follow the green track between drystone walls ahead, which ends after 100 yards. Then take the stone squeeze stile ahead. After a further stile you should take the field gate ahead, then continue until you reach the road opposite a cricket pitch.

❹ Turn right along the road towards the hamlet of West Morton. After passing High Ash Farm and Applegate Barn on your right take the first track on your left and follow it downhill past Brownhill Bungalow.

❺ After 250 yards, take the wooden gate between Dene Farm and Dene Hole Farm to pass a barn with an inscription 'WSW 1913', then take another gate and follow the left-hand side of the field downhill.

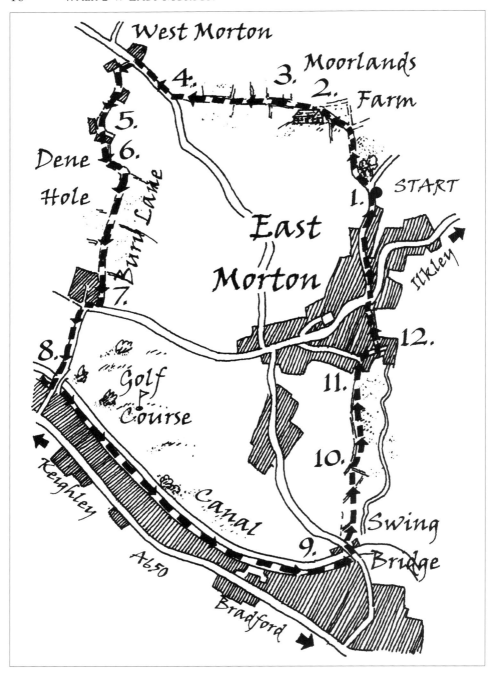

## PLACES of INTEREST

Nearby **East Riddlesden Hall** is a rambling 17th-century National Trust Property, complete with ghosts and grounds which include a huge 16th-century tithe barn and a large pond where fish were reared for the monks of Bolton Abbey. (For information on opening times, telephone: 01535 607075.) **Cliff Castle**, Keighley, is part high Victorian mill-owners' mansion and part museum of natural history and local interest, including one of the best geology exhibits to be found anywhere between Edinburgh and London (tel: 01535 758230). And it's still free!

❻ This brings you to the top end of a track called Bury Lane on your left. Follow this track, which shortly turns downhill to the right. (The footpath that leaves the lane at this bend goes towards a spot 150 yards away where, according to the OS map, there are cup-marked boulders. I found large boulders built into the wall but I couldn't make out the markings.)

❼ Follow the Bury Lane footpath downhill until you come out on a road near houses. Turn right and then left down Swine Lane towards the canal bridge. There is no pavement on this stretch of the road, so keep to the right and take care on the narrow bridge.

❽ After crossing the bridge turn right down the ramp to the towpath, then sharp right again back under the bridge and follow the towpath until, after ¾ mile, you come to the next bridge, a swing bridge.

*The Leeds and Liverpool Canal.*

❾ Cross the swing bridge and, after 20 yards, squeeze through the gap in the wall to take the footpath on your right. This takes you down a few stone steps, along a tarmac path, and to a stone stile by an old elm stump.

❿ Cross the bumpy pasture ahead, keeping fairly close to the wall on the left at the top of the slope.

⓫ When the next stile returns you to the village, take the road ahead for a short distance, then turn right at the next junction by a triangle of grass.

⓬ A few yards further on, opposite the sign for Cliffe Mill Fold, walk up the cobbled driveway to your left. This leads to a footpath which takes you, via an iron gate, to more passageways amongst the stone-built houses of the village. You will eventually come out of Little Lane onto the main street opposite stone steps that take you up to Green End Lane and the start of the walk.

# ADEL

*Length: 6 miles*

| **Getting there**: Follow signs for Adel from the A660 Otley Road, Leeds. | **Parking**: There is a small layby opposite Adel church. Alternatively, start the walk at Golden Acre Park, which has its own car park. | **Maps**: OS Explorer 27 Lower Wharfedale and OS Pathfinder 683 Leeds (GR 273402). |
| --- | --- | --- |

Not yet engulfed by the suburbs of Leeds, the stone cottages of the old country village of Adel can still be found, tucked away not far from the historic church and the village cricket ground. Adel sits right on the edge of open countryside with long easy walks across field and fairway, through bluebell woods and along craggy slopes clad in birch and oak with patches of heather and

bilberry. We even saw a fox. The flight path of the Leeds Bradford airport might be close by, but so are heron and the wildfowl on Paul's Pond and the Park lake.

Adel church had its origins in the 12th century, in the turbulent times of King Stephen and Matilda, the Empress Maud. The nave and porch date from about 1170. The elaborate carvings above the Norman

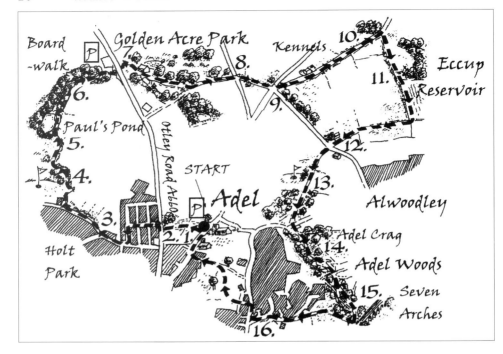

arch are, literally, a revelation, with the lion, the calf, the creature with 'a face as a man' and the eagle taken from the fourth chapter of the Book of Revelations. Inside the church there are salamanders and dragons amongst more familiar figures. Imagine the fresh carving in its original colours and you've got something near to the ritual drama of a Mayan temple.

Breary Marsh, which you cross via a boardwalk, is the best remaining example of a wet-valley alderwood in West Yorkshire. Wilderness and wet are in short supply in this part of the county and amongst the alders you'll see an uncommon plant, shaggy clumps of the great tussock sedge, described by David Bellamy as 'the original gonk' (if you remember what gonks were). Look out for marsh marigold,

valerian and woody nightshade, orange-tip butterflies and six-spot burnet moths, long-tailed tits, bramblings, goldfinches, chiff chaffs and blackcaps.

The attractions of Golden Acre Park include Blenheim Courtyard glasshouses and demonstration gardens where the *Gardening Which?* experts conduct trials of fruit, vegetables and flowers. There's something for everyone and the small trial gardens develop new, and old, ideas that could be applied to any garden. Harry Ramsden's heather garden provides colour throughout the year.

The Walk

❶ Take the old stone stile opposite the church gate. Follow the footpath between fields, through another stone stile, then

**FOOD and DRINK**

The café in Golden Acre Park is just the place to take a break on this walk. The Lawnswood Arms on the Otley Road near Adel is a Big Steak Pub, complete with a Wacky Warehouse for the children. It does not serve just steaks of course; the menu includes mushroom dipper and Sambar satay. Telephone: 0113 267 1823. The Parkway Hotel, next to Golden Acre Park, offers lunches, evening meals and bar meals, and, if you're staying overnight there's the added attraction of the leisure club, with swimming pool and jacuzzi...the perfect way to unwind after an arduous ramble.

cross the middle of the next field. *Warning*: a set of stone steps at the end of this field brings you out abruptly at the edge of the busy A660 Otley Road.

❷ Cross the Otley Road, turn right, then look for a footpath between nos 549 and 551. Carry on straight along the length of Kingsley Road then, at the T-junction, turn left along Kingsley Avenue. At the next junction, with Holt Lane, turn right, passing a housing development on your right on Adel Meadows.

❸ Turn right along Holt Lane. Stay on the narrow road, passing a children's play area, and after about 400 yards take the public footpath on your right, just before the driveway to 'The Barn'.

❹ Follow the yellow posts across the golf course; the path follows the right-hand edge of the course towards Fish Pond Plantation. Old Cookridge Hall, now a leisure centre, stands on the slope to the left. The forestry authority is planting new woodland at the edge of the course.

❺ On entering Fish Pond Plantation, take the right hand path ahead to pass Paul's Pond on your left. At the end of the pond go down the banking and take the path marked 'Leeds Country Way' across a railway-sleeper footbridge, just before a gate at the edge of the wood.

❻ The path follows a drystone wall at the edge of the wood and then joins a bridleway. Follow the bridleway to the right and, after a few yards, take the path that forks to the left. This takes you over the Breary Marsh boardwalk.

At the end of the boardwalk turn right at the car park and go through the stone arch under the Otley Road.

❼ On emerging in Golden Acre Park, turn left and follow broad paths, past the café and toilets, enjoying the flowerbeds and parklands on the northern slopes of the lake as you go.

Near the lower corner of the lake, at a T-junction of paths, follow the bridleway to the left, along the edge of the park.

❽ At the end of the bridleway cross the road to enter King Lane and follow this, keeping to the path on the narrow verge, to the junction known as Five Lane Ends.

❾ At Five Lane Ends take the second opening on your left, Eccup Moor Road, part of the Leeds Country Way. You then pass the kennels of the National Canine Defence League on your left.

❿ After ½ mile, opposite a copse, take the footpath on your right, part of the Leeds to Ilkley link of the Dales Way. It follows a hawthorn hedge on the right; Eccup reservoir lies amongst the trees to the left.

**⓫** Two stiles take the path along the edge of Goodrick Plantation, then, back in open fields, the path follows a wire fence on the right. At the next stile turn right, again following the Dales Way link.

**⓬** At the top of this field a stile takes you onto a golf practice range. Follow the wire fence on the left to a track which brings you back to King Lane.

Cross the road and take the public bridleway ahead, marked 'Meanwood Valley Trail'. The path follows the edge of Headingley golf course with views of Leeds Bradford airport and its main flight path

and, in the dip to the right, Bramhope. As the sign says: 'Please beware of golf balls from the right'.

**⓭** After passing through a wooden gate into a field look for a gate and stile 200 yards on your left, again marked 'Dales Way'. Take this and follow the path half-right down into scrubby ash and oak woodland.

Cross Stairfoot Lane next to a small car park and go forward through the gates onto a bridleway.

After 50 yards there is a short detour to Adel Crag (which reminds me of a sphinx). You can rejoin the main path via another short path.

*The church of St John the Baptist at Adel.*

**PLACES of INTEREST**

**Tropical World**, at Canal Gardens, Roundhay, Leeds, now attracts over a million visitors a year; it houses the largest collection of tropical plants outside Kew Gardens. There are birdwing butterflies, fruit bats, bush babies, piranhas and sea cucumbers. It is well worth a visit (tel: 0113 266 1850).

⓮ Back on the main path turn left (that is, keep heading in the same direction) and you soon come to a triangular clearing. Take the path that forks along the right-hand edge of the clearing, signed 'the Dales Way' and 'Meanwood Valley Trail'.

The path descends into Adel Woods amongst hollies and oaks. Keep on the main path and don't turn off left on the little path by the Old Leodeosians' sports ground.

After 150 yards there is a small round pond on the right; the path continues down rough steps and, in a gully, crosses a clapper bridge made of two huge slabs of sandstone. Cross the footpath ahead. A few yards further on there is a small stone arch, lined with moss and liverwort, over a little spring on the left.

Stay on the footpath along the wooded valley side – don't branch off right down towards the beck. There are old ponds down in the valley bottom.

⓯ On reaching the Seven Arches, an old aqueduct, follow the path to the right, in front of the arches, cross Meanwood Beck, and, as you reach the top of the slope, take a well-defined bridleway which branches sharply to the right.

Follow this bridleway onwards, past beech trees on your right, then between pastures until you emerge on a bend of Tile Lane. Turn left, passing a 1930s semi-detached house.

⓰ After passing Adel primary school on the left, keep on the left-hand pavement and after 300 yards, just past a bus stop, cross Sir George Martin Drive to turn right along Long Causeway.

⓱ In 400 yards, after passing Manor House Croft, turn left into Wayland Drive, a cul-de-sac. In the top left-hand corner, between Wayland Court and Wayland Close, take a short path which brings you out onto Bedquilts recreation grounds.

Head across the playing fields towards the diagonally opposite corner to find a kissing-gate to a path between gardens that brings you out on a lane. After passing some of the oldest cottages in Adel turn right along on Church Lane, passing the old school, the war memorial and memorial hall on your return to the church.

# HAREWOOD

*Length: 3¼ miles*

| **Getting there**: Harewood lies on the A61, 7 miles north of Leeds. There is a bus every half hour from Leeds and Harrogate. | **Parking**: More or less limited to the A659 Collingham Road, opposite the park gates. It is best to park on the opposite side to the post office to avoid obstructing traffic approaching the lights. | **Map**: OS Explorer 27 Lower Wharfedale (GR 322452). |
| --- | --- | --- |

Harewood is a perfect example of an estate village. Built in local sandstone, it has kept its harmonious look with a pleasingly uniform style. As is fitting, the most splendid architecture in the village is reserved for the Park's archway lodge.

At the start of this walk the view of the ancient holloway of Fitts Lane, with a broad expanse of Wharfedale framed by trees, is more reminiscent of the work of Constable than of Turner, who painted locally. In 1797 Turner, then aged 22, was invited to Harewood by Edward Lascelles. *Harewood House from the North-East*, a watercolour purchased for ten guineas, still hangs in the house. In this painting Turner

### FOOD and DRINK

The stone-built Harewood Arms Hotel is open all day for food and offers ensuite accommodation. Telephone: 0113 288 6566. There is a café in the grounds of the Park. Harewood's post office/village shop is opposite the gates to the Park.

first began to move away from architectural studies towards the landscape itself.

This short walk takes in part of the Ebor Way alongside the River Wharfe and returns through Harewood's North Park.

THE WALK

❶ Head out of the village on the A61 Harrogate Road. The pavement runs out as you leave the village, but it is possible to stick to the grass verge most of the way. Just before the road curves left, step into Fitts Lane, a farm track on your right. It becomes a holloway, a sunken lane, as it descends towards the River Wharfe.

❷ As Fitts Lane swings right at the River Wharfe, take the riverside footpath alongside the field on your left. After ¼ mile leave the field edge and cross a silted-up channel near an old sandstone chimney, so that you stay close to the river bank. Continue for another ½ mile. When you get to within 200 yards of Harewood Bridge start looking for a path down nearer to the riverside.

❸ At a gap in the stone wall near Harewood Bridge, cross the A61 and descend to cross the timberyard of

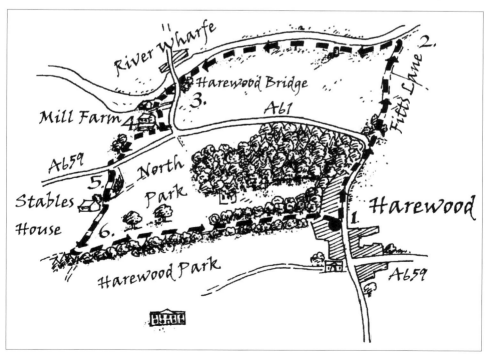

Harewood Bridge Sawmill. Head towards the farm buildings. The stile is behind the sawmill office on your left.

❹ Turn left along the farm access road to start making a semicircle around the farm, keeping the buildings to your right. A short distance along the access road, take a stile by a gate on your right. Turn right and head for the gate. On entering the next field turn right to continue around the farm. Keep fairly close to the right-hand side of this field, heading towards a row of trees. As the field narrows you'll find a stile in the far corner.

❺ At the A659 Otley Road turn right and, after 50 yards, take the bridleway on the left which is the driveway to Stables House Stud Farm. Follow this up the slope until, after ¼ mile, you reach a crossroads of bridleways.

❻ Turn left and go along the lane, which follows the boundary wall of the Harewood estate on your right, back towards the village and the start of the walk.

*Archway Lodge, Harewood Park.*

# BRAMHAM

*Length: 4½ miles*

| Getting there: Bramham lies alongside the A1, 3½ miles south of Wetherby. | Parking: On the road near the centre of the village. | Map: OS Pathfinder 673 Tadcaster (GR 425429). |
|---|---|---|

Bramham, nestling in a hollow in the hills, with its ancient oval churchyard and its old inns, is more peaceful now that it is bypassed by the A1. Bramham's position on this ancient thoroughfare to the north brought it to the forefront of history on several occasions. The Romans came this way, the Percy Rebellion was finally crushed in the Battle of Bramham Moor, 1408, and victims of the Cromwellian Civil War lie in the churchyard. The large oval shape of the churchyard suggests that it is Celtic, with its origins in the 6th-century British kingdom of Elmet.

The Red Lion inn by a stream in the village centre is a reminder of coaching days, as is the outline of a horse, dated 1700, on the wall of a former public house opposite.

Headley Hall, south of the village, is an

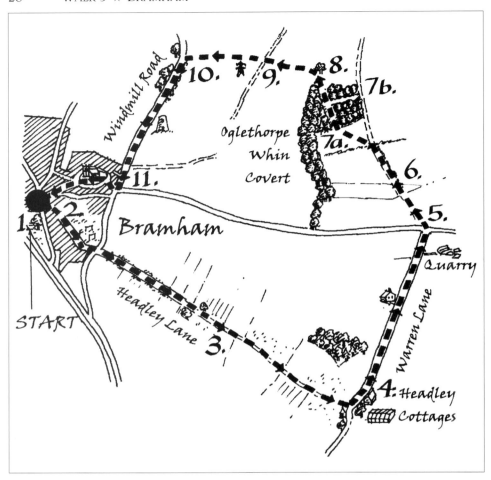

experimental farm run by Leeds University. On this walk look out for experiments in agro-forestry, where crops are grown beneath planted trees. And on a clear day, be sure to linger over the wonderful view from Oglethorpe woods, from where you can see the white horse of Kilburn on the slopes of the North York Moors ahead.

Bramham man Levi Whitehead, who died aged 100 in 1787, was the fastest man in England in his day. He ran 4 miles in 19 minutes and at the age of 96 he still walked at 4 miles an hour. You are welcome to take a little longer over the following walk!

THE WALK

❶ From the war memorial climb Almshouse Hill, which zigzags up opposite the Red Lion.

❷ At the top continue on the lane, now called Freely Lane, passing the entrance to

**④** At the end of the track, with Headley Hall ahead, turn left, passing Headley Cottages on your right, and continue on Warren Lane for ¼ mile.

**⑤** At the T-junction with York Lane, part of a Roman road, take the footpath opposite and slightly to the left by the double metal gates marked 'Private Road to Oglethorpe Hall Farm'. The footpath veers slightly left up the slope across open fields.

**⑥** On a clear day from this vantage point, Oglethorpe Woods, just 200 feet above sea level, you can see the white horse of Kilburn on the slopes of the North York Moors ahead and the Wolds to the north-east, both some 25 miles away.

---

**FOOD and DRINK**

The Red Lion offers home-cooked foods every lunchtime and evening. Telephone: 01937 843524. The White Horse has occasional barbecues. Bramham post office doubles as off licence and newsagent.

---

Bramham ambulance service on your right and a children's play area on your left. At the end of the lane, near the high limestone walls of Bramham Hall on your right, continue onwards across the road along the straight lane ahead, Headley Lane.

**❸** Ignore the public footpath to the left after ¼ mile. After ½ mile the lane becomes a farm track. Continue for another ½ mile.

*Bramham churchyard.*

---

**PLACES of INTEREST**

**Bramham Park** stately home has extensive grounds where horse trials are occasionally held. **Tadcaster** dates back to Roman times, and John Smith's and Samuel Smith's breweries stand by the River Wharfe.

---

**❼** You have a choice ahead:

(a) When you reach the field next to a large plantation (Oglethorpe Whin Covert) ahead, take the official public footpath, which heads away from the lane to the left at an angle of 45 degrees, to reach the wood at the right-hand end of the first big block of conifers, 200 yards left of the lane. From here the poorly defined footpath crosses the wood. *Or*

(b) Since the wood can be rather overgrown with nettles at this point you may prefer to take the unofficial detour, at present apparently favoured by the landowners. Continue on the lane down the right-hand side of the plantation. After 100 yards look for a footpath along a narrow woodland ride to your left. Follow this into the wood for 200 yards to rejoin the official footpath which you should follow to the right to the edge of the wood.

**❽** On leaving the wood head half-left towards a large oak, then turn left, heading slightly to the right of the nearest electricity pylon in the direction of Clifford with its two churches. Look for marker posts and a stile in the hedge.

**❾** Step through the hedge, cross Heygate Lane and continue on the footpath opposite across the fields.

**❿** After 500 yards, when the footpath comes out on Windmill Road, turn left and follow the road back past the windmill to the village.

**⓫** At the T-junction with Toulston Lane turn right, then take the next right, Vicarage Lane, down the hill. Cross the large oval churchyard and, leaving by the lychgate, take the lane ahead back to the start of the walk.

Windmill Road
Bramham

# BARWICK IN ELMET

*Length: 4¾ miles*

| | | |
|---|---|---|
| **Getting there**: Barwick lies between Leeds, the A64(T) and the A1, just north of Garforth. | **Parking**: On the road in the village. | **Map**: OS Pathfinder 683 Leeds (GR 400375). |

Looking at Barwick's maypole, its fine old pubs and church, you'd guess that it was a village with a long history. You'd be right; at the start of this walk the street called the Boyle curves around the bailey, the outermost wall, of a 12th-century Norman fort. But the settlement at Barwick is even older than that for the Normans built their castle on the site of an Iron Age hill-fort.

The village's commanding position comes courtesy of a natural ridge of magnesian limestone. Barwick is on a geological boundary and you'll see both limestone and coal measures sandstone in the village buildings. All Saints church, for instance, has a sandstone porch and limestone tower.

Barwick's lofty maypole has caused some traditional rivalry amongst the local villages. Every three years it is taken down

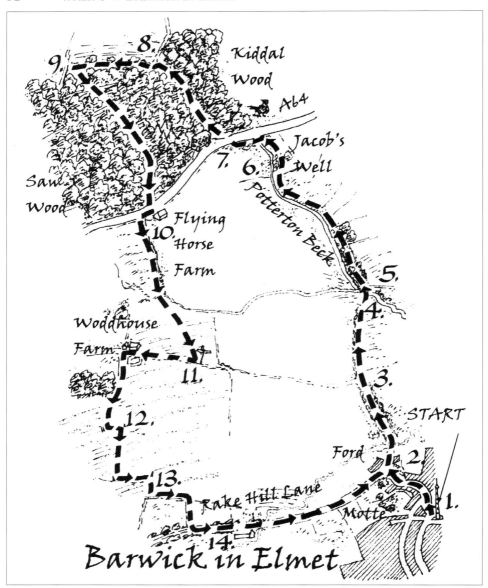

and repainted amid great ceremony. Some years ago, however, Aberford succeeded in kidnapping the pole. Happily it is now back in its rightful place again.

This walk includes a variety of woodland and farmland, including one wide open expanse of arable land with views stretching from the tower blocks of

## FOOD and DRINK

The Black Swan, near the church, serves family lunches from 12 to 2 pm. The menu includes lasagne, pies, fillet of fish and a giant Yorkshire dinner. Telephone: 0113 281 3065. The Gascoigne Arms, next to the Maypole, also offers freshly prepared food. At the other end of the main street the New Inn has pub food available at lunchtime. The Copper Kettle teashop on the main street is closed Tuesday afternoons and all day Monday. The Pizza Piccante takeaway is nearby and there's a fish and chip shop on the Boyle, strategically situated at the corner of the Norman bailey. Halfway around this walk a red double-decker bus serves as a roadside café in the layby at Kiddal Bridge. Anyone for a bacon sandwich?

Seacroft to the white horse of Kilburn.

THE WALK

❶ With the Black Swan and church behind you, leave the main street at the maypole and Gascoigne Arms, then follow the Boyle down to the right. Look out for the motte, which was crowned with a timber keep, between the bungalows on your left.

❷ At the bottom of the slope, where the road swings sharply left to become Rakehill Road, turn right down a lane in front of houses and cross the stream by a footbridge next to the ford.

❸ In 400 yards, where the lane turns left into a field, take the footpath ahead which keeps close to the hedge on your left.

❹ At the end of the hedge line continue ahead over the field to cross the footbridge over the stream.

❺ Cross the stile on your left and follow the path alongside Potterton Beck on your left. At first this runs alongside trees then, after crossing two stiles, it continues to follow the stream along the left-hand side of a field.

❻ A further stile brings you into a field adjacent to the A64. The path skirts around a tree-filled hollow marked Jacob's Well on the OS map. By the road a stile takes you left into a roadside copse, emerging after 100 yards opposite a layby.

❼ Cross with care and take the footpath almost directly opposite into the wood.

❽ At the far side of the wood, at the corner of a field, ignore the footpath gate to the Leeds Country Way ahead and turn sharp left to cross a railway-sleeper bridge over a ditch. Then take the path that keeps you closest to the edge of the wood on your right.

❾ In 500 yards, just before you reach a drainage ditch and a lane at the corner of the wood, turn sharp left to follow a footpath back into the wood. This footpath continues more or less straight through the wood for 600 yards, then veers to the right (waymarked at the time of writing). In a further 250 yards you emerge from a dense hedge at the side of the A64 opposite Flying Horse Farm.

❿ Cross the road, turn right, and, in 50 yards, take the public footpath on your left over a stone stile. You pass oak trees and then follow a hawthorn hedge on your left down the side of the next field. In the left-hand corner cross the stile by the metal

**PLACES of INTEREST**

The best free attraction in the area is **Lotherton Hall**, near the Garforth junction of the A1. It has a picnic area, shop, café, deer park and an excellent bird garden (tel: 0113 281 3723). The South American condors are particularly impressive. **Leeds** has the **Royal Armouries**, **Art Gallery** and **Museums**, and **Temple Newsam House**.

gate. The footpath now goes straight ahead up the slope; there should be a signpost at the top to aim at.

❶ At the signpost turn sharp right to Woodhouse Farm. You pass through a gate as you reach the farm. Immediately after passing the buildings on your right, take the public footpath along the track on your left, passing through another gate into a field and then past the end of a belt of trees on your right. There are wide open views as far as Ferrybridge and Drax power stations,

York and the white horse of Kilburn, with the tower blocks of Seacroft on your right.

❷ Two hundred yards after passing the wood there is a post, and precious little else, to tell you where to turn left (east). In a further 100 yards another post directs you to turn sharp right (south). In another 200 yards it's left (east) again, then 150 yards and sharp right (south) towards the first hedge, after a mile of zigzagging over open fields.

❸ Turn left and follow the hawthorn hedge on your right, heading east towards Barwick church tower for 200 yards, then turn right through a wooden squeeze stile, over a little railway-sleeper bridge and along the right-hand side of the next field.

❹ Turn left on Rake Hill Lane, a wide green track between hedges, and follow this back to the Boyle and the start of the walk.

# LEDSHAM

*Length: 4½ miles*

**Getting there**: Ledsham lies close to the A1, east of its junction with the A63(T) Monk Fryston road.

**Parking**: Limited to a few spaces on Park Lane, opposite the Chequers public house. An alternative is to start this walk from the RSPB Fairburn Ings Reserve car park on Newton Lane between Fairburn and Allerton Bywater.

**Map**: OS Pathfinder 693 Castleford and Pontefract (GR 298457).

Ledsham is a classic English country village nestling in a hollow by a limestone ridge. Its Saxon church is probably the oldest standing building in West Yorkshire. Around the church cluster almshouses, working farms, the old village school and an unspoiled country pub.

Like many villages, it once had its witches. In Tudor times Mary Pannel is said to have cast a spell which caused the death of the son of the local landowner, Henry Witham. Even Dame Mary Bolles, whose life-size shrouded effigy (1662) lies in Ledsham church, was reputed to have

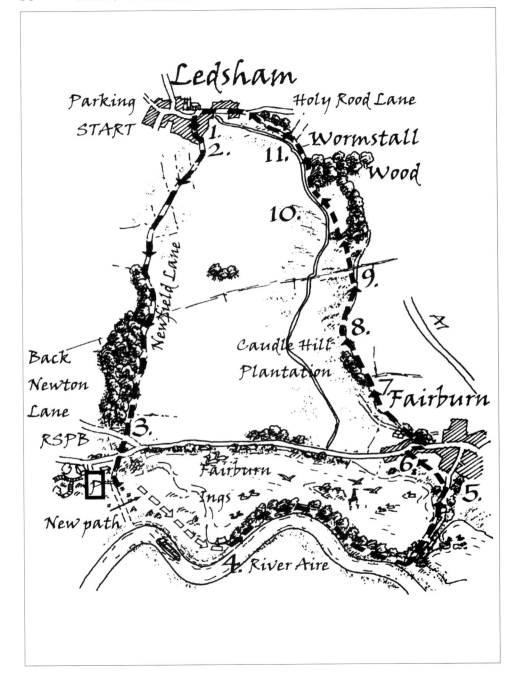

Ledsham

Parking
START

Holy Rood Lane

1.
2.

11.

Wormstall
Wood

10

Newfield Lane

9.

8.

7 Fairburn

Back
Newton
Lane

RSPB

3.

Caudle Hill
Plantation

6

5.

New path

Fairburn

Ings

4. River Aire

**FOOD and DRINK**

The menu at the Chequers Inn, Ledsham, includes home-made soup, smoked mackerel, smoked salmon scrambled, chocolate roulade and sticky toffee pudding with custard. Please note: this pub has a six-day licence and it is not open on Sundays. Telephone: 01977 683135. At the White Horse Inn in neighbouring Ledston, fish is a speciality.

dabbled in the black arts. In contrast, Lady Betty of Ledston Hall (d. 1739), who reclines elegantly nearby, reading her book, is remembered for her good works. 'To behold her is an immediate check to loose behaviour', wrote Richard Steele in *The Tatler*, 'and to love her is a liberal education'. She founded scholarships at Oxford, a school and orphanage in the village, and contributed to the Sir John Lewis's almshouses which still stand behind the church.

The church dates back to around 700. There is an Anglo-Saxon archway (with Victorian carving) at the bottom of the tower, with a Norman belfry added above. At least one piece of Roman masonry was built into the tower, inside the church: a stone with a butcher's cleaver carved on it, from a Roman altar.

This walk has a splendid view across the length of West Yorkshire from the limestone ridge. Thanks to a new path provided by RJB Mining across a reclaimed coal tip, the walk makes a full circuit of the Fairburn Ings lake. This RSPB reserve has a picnic area, boardwalks, hides and 2 miles of paths. Remember your binoculars.

Ledsham holds an annual fair, around the first weekend in September.

THE WALK

❶ From Ledsham church take the lane that leaves the main road through the village at the south-east corner of the churchyard.

❷ Follow this out of the village, passing the entrance to a cul-de-sac on your right as the lane curves to the left. The track becomes a footpath as it crosses open fields and, after ½ mile, passes along the edge of a plantation.

❸ On emerging on Back Newton Lane take the short track ahead (which is not a public footpath) towards the entrance to the RSPB Fairburn Ings Reserve car park. There are boardwalks to explore to your right but the walk continues along a new path* on your left which takes you across a landscaped area which was formerly a colliery dump. The main lake is over to your left. In about ½ mile you'll meet a footpath along the north bank of the River Aire.

*At the time of writing the new path had yet to open and walkers had to take an unofficial route along the gated track ahead, then turn left at the river.

❹ Turn left along the riverside path for ¾ mile, then, after descending a slope, turn left on the track which runs between the two lakes of the reserve. Birds seen from the hides include whooper, bewick and mute swan (the first two in winter only), cormorant, great crested grebe and plenty of black-headed gulls.

❺ After leaving the lake shore, in 150 yards take the footpath on the left and

## PLACES of INTEREST

**Castleford**, to the south of Ledsham, is an unpretentious little town with a history spanning 2,000 years. It is where Henry Moore was first encouraged to take up carving. The primary school now named after him still has his earliest work, a memorial to the pupils of the school who died in the First World War (not open to the public). **Castleford Library** in the centre of the town has a local studies collection and a museum room. To see **Leventhorpe Vineyard**, Britain's most northerly commercial vineyard with its own winery, turn off the A642 at the Bridge Farm Hotel between Woodlesford and Swillington. The winery is behind Leventhorpe Cottages on the left. If you would like to taste the three whites and the red produced here, visit on Saturdays between 11 am and 5 pm or on Sundays between 12 noon and 5 pm (tel: 0113 288 9088). The quick-draining, south-facing slope is reasonably frost-free, sheltered by a belt of trees beside the canal and river.

follow it parallel to the shore until it emerges amongst the houses on Newton Lane.

❻ Turn right along the road and climb the hill for 100 yards, then take a lane which turns sharply to the left by the trees on the crest of the ridge. After 100 yards follow the footpath which branches right along a track.

❼ Follow the footpath across a field and along behind Caudle Hill Plantation.

On a clear day you can see the length of West Yorkshire, from the county border by the RSPB car park to Holme Moss on the crest of the Pennines. You are standing on a ridge of magnesian limestone, looking across the coal measures towards the millstone grit of the South Pennines.

❽ The next stile after the plantation brings you out onto the slopes of a little valley, the path initially following the fence on your right. Traces of strip cultivation can be seen on the slope ahead.

❾ Just before you get to the overhead pylon wires, by a couple of thorn trees, take the path forking down to the left. Cross the belt of trees ahead using the two stiles.

❿ Follow the path across the next field, which is bordered on three sides by Wormstall Wood, heading for the bottom corner of the next block of trees ahead. Continue with the wood on the right and Ledsham Beck on your left until a stile by a gate takes you onto a farm track.

⓫ After leaving the wood and crossing a second stile by a gate, leave the track and follow the footpath back to the village. There is a row of mature beeches to your right. A kissing-gate brings you out on Holy Rood Lane. Turn left towards the church.

# HIGH ACKWORTH

*Length: 5½ miles*

| **Getting there**: High Ackworth is on the A628, 2 miles south of Pontefract. | **Parking**: There is room to park on the road on the church side of the little village green at High Ackworth. | **Map**: OS Pathfinder 704 Hemsworth (GR 441180). |
| --- | --- | --- |

This walk from the pleasant little village of High Ackworth will take you back in time to the 17th century, to the days of daring highwaymen and terrifying, devastating outbreaks of the plague.

Ackworth Old Hall, at the end of this walk, built in the early 1600s, has a rugged, romantic look that is lacking in later, more elegant, mansions. The ghost of the highwayman John Nevison is said to haunt

the Hall. He used to hide in a compartment above the main entrance. Nevison was born in Pontefract in 1639 and in 1676 he made his ride, often attributed to the later Dick Turpin, from Gad's Hill, London, to York, covering the 190 miles in 15 hours.

Ackworth plague stone, which stands outside the village on the Pontefract road, is associated with the outbreak of plague in 1645. The hollow was intended to hold

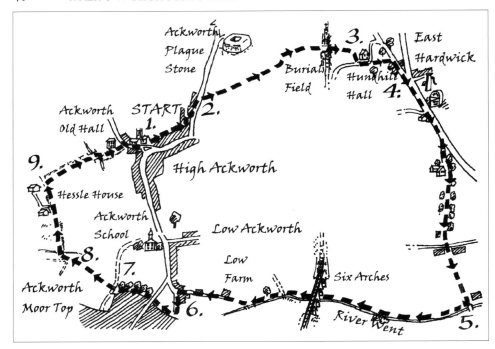

vinegar to disinfect coins used in payment for supplies left at the boundaries. This walk crosses the Burial Field, where plague victims were laid to rest.

The Quaker School at Ackworth was originally built as a hospital in 1747. Gainsborough, Hogarth and Handel helped with the fundraising appeal. The Society of Friends opened it as a school in 1779. In the early days the boy and girl boarders often stayed for several years without visiting their homes.

There is some excellent easy walking on this route, but take care around the Burial Field where the waymarking is not too clear.

THE WALK

❶ From the village green find the footpath heading north-east, to the *right* of the Georgian stone-built Manor House. Continue on this footpath, crossing a stone-sett stile and following a field edge, until you enter a cul-de-sac, Woodland Grove. Turn left, then right along Meadow Way, to emerge on the A628 Pontefract road. Turn left but start looking for a footpath sign and steps amongst the trees and hedging opposite, just before you get to a house called 'Tall Trees'.

❷ The steps take you out onto open fields. Continue in the same direction for almost ½ mile, crossing three small plank bridges until the footpath kinks to the left around the boundary of the Burial Field, where victims of the 17th-century plague were interred. Follow this boundary and you

**FOOD and DRINK**

The speciality at the Brown Cow near the start of this walk is all types of beef – roast joints and steaks are prepared on the premises. Lunches are served from 12 noon to 2 pm. Telephone: 01977 704735. The Rustic Arms, by the railway bridge on the road to East Hardwick, overlooks its own little boating and fishing lake. Telephone: 01977 794136.

❸ Swing right with the path at the garden walls of Hundhill Hall, to come out on Hundhill Lane. Follow the lane just as far as the sharp left bend, then take three stone steps to cross the wall opposite. After 200 yards this footpath emerges on Sandy Gate Lane at a row of horse chestnut trees. Turn right past the cricket pitch and continue until this perfect English country lane emerges abruptly at the busy A639 Pontefract to Doncaster road, opposite East Hardwick village pump.

❹ Follow the A639 right, to the south-east, for 800 yards. There are grass verges only, so take care. The cast-iron mile post was made in Liversedge. Ignore Station Road on your right, signed to Ackworth,

soon turn a right corner and start veering back to your original direction. When you get to the crest of the rise, head east for Hundhill Hall, with the ridge of magnesian limestone rising behind it. Cross a bridge over a deep, ferny railway cutting, in coal-measures sandstone.

*Ackworth Old Hall.*

---

### PLACES of INTEREST

**Pontefract Castle** was the last stronghold of the Royalists in the English Civil War. They held out until two months after the execution of King Charles. You can still see initials carved by Civil War prisoners held in the magazine beneath the castle. In 1400 Henry IV had the imprisoned Richard II murdered here. For opening times, telephone 01977 723440. **Pontefract Museum** in the centre of the town traces the history of liquorice, which was once grown in the area. Licquorice allsorts and pontefract cakes are still made in the town. Telephone: 01977 722741. **Brockadale Yorkshire Wildlife Trust Reserve** at **Wentbridge** lies in a narrow valley cut through the limestone ridge. There are extensive woods and meadows rich in wild flowers.

---

and in another 200 yards take the next right into Whitegate Lane. After 200 yards, leave the lane, now the driveway to the Manse, and take the footpath to the left, behind the hedge. Follow this for ¾ mile, crossing Rigg Lane at Low Grange Farm until, near Ackworth waste water treatment works, you come to a low concrete bridge over the little River Went. There is a small packhorse bridge to the left.

❺ Don't cross the river but follow the footpath on your right, close to its north bank, for as far as you can, passing under the 'six arches' railway viaduct. Ignore Tan House Lane to the right and, still keeping to the riverside, cross an iron girder bridge and a stile. Eventually, at a stone bridge, the path veers right, away from the river, towards the buildings of Low Farm. Pass close to the farm buildings on your right

and follow Low Farm Lane towards Low Ackworth village.

❻ On joining Mill Lane turn left, then cross the recreation ground to reach the far corner. Cross the main road near a bus stop and look for a footpath opposite signed down to the right, cross a stile over a concrete fence, then follow the path left in a belt of trees which runs between houses and the fields surrounding Ackworth school.

❼ On emerging at a lane to Ackworth school, take the public footpath which runs along the track opposite.

❽ After 400 yards, at a crossroads of footpaths, follow the lane to the right. Cross Hessle Beck on your right and continue up the slope towards Hessle House. As soon as you reach the farm buildings, take the turning on your right into a field, then immediately turn left, to continue onwards with the hawthorn hedge on your left.

❾ On reaching a stile by the next set of farm buildings, turn right along a footpath and head for High Ackworth church on the skyline. Cross a concrete bridge out of the field and continue up the hill towards Ackworth Old Hall, crossing the stile on your right after about 30 yards. Continue up the long, narrow field towards a stone step and flagstone stile in the top left corner.

Turn right along Purston Lane back to the village green.

# NOTTON

## *Length: 5 or 3½ miles*

Getting there: Notton lies 1 mile east of the A61 between Wakefield and Barnsley.

Parking: Around (but not on) the village green.

Map: OS Pathfinder 703 Wakefield (South) (GR 351131).

Notton is mentioned in the Domesday Book of 1086. It features some sturdy old stone-built houses, three of them listed buildings, but it is the large village green which gives Notton an identity all its own. Drovers taking their cattle south paid a halfpenny per head for a night's grazing on Notton village green. Smawell Lane, a roadside nature reserve at the start of this walk, is still sometimes referred to as Ha'penny Lane, suggesting that it was the original drove road into the village.

An annual gala is held on the green, which was purchased for £5 in 1949 and, though privately owned, is preserved as common land.

Between Wakefield and Barnsley lies a belt of countryside famous for its country parks: Nostell Priory, Bretton, Woolley and Cannon Hall. On this walk we visit

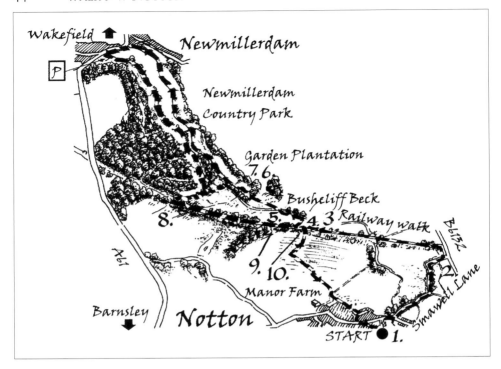

Newmillerdam, part of the estate of Chevet Hall, once home of the Pilkington family.

Notton has a listed monument to the railway age: a bridge designed by George Stephenson. The walk includes a panoramic railway walk along what was a branch line of the Midland Railway. It was opened in 1905 to link London with Glasgow, via the Settle-Carlisle line. It got only as far as Dewsbury but was never busy and closed with the Beeching cuts of the 1960s. Apple trees on the embankment are a reminder of train crews who chucked apple cores from the cabs of their steam engines.

An alternative to the full walk is to follow the footpath through Applehaigh Clough from the south-east corner of the green to visit Notton Woods, now managed by Wakefield Countryside Service.

THE WALK

❶ Leave Notton village green by the north-east corner. After crossing Gill Bridge turn left into Smawell Lane.

❷ Follow this quiet, winding lane for ½ mile (but keep an eye out for the odd car); then, 10 yards before joining the B6132 Chevet to Royston road, turn into the small car park on your left. At the back of the car park descend to join the railway walk to your left, along the old cutting. The cutting opens out and turns into a high embankment with panoramas towards Woolley on your left and Chevet stables on

**FOOD and DRINK**

The Oliver Twist on the B6132, ½ mile east of the village green, is a popular family pub. More traditional surroundings are provided at Newmillerdam at the Fox and Hounds (telephone: 01924 255474) and at The Dam Inn which has a large restaurant (telephone: 01924 255625); both offer extensive menus lunchtime and evening. The Beuley Café stands between the two, overlooking the dam. Back at the start of the walk, Notton post office and village store is, at the time of writing, renowned for its bacon sandwiches.

your right. Embankment flowers include knapweed, viper's bugloss, wild mignonette and heather.

❸ Before you get to the bridge that crosses

over the line, as the railway walk ahead changes from embankment to cutting, turn off on the alternative route signed up the slope to your right.

❹ Follow the farm track for 40 or 50 yards past the bridge, and a slope with birch and bracken on your left. Before you get to the sign 'To Barnsley Road', take the small path to your right, down the embankment, marked 'Motorcycles and horses strictly prohibited'.

❺ This path turns to the left to follow Bushcliff Beck. Take the narrow stone bridge by the stone gatepost across the beck, where stickleback and mayfly nymphs live among the pondweed.

*Manor Farm House, passed on the walk.*

---

**PLACES of INTEREST**

At the **Waterton Discovery Centre**, **Anglers Country Park**, between Crofton and Ryhill, (tel. 01924 303980) the 'ghost' of Victorian naturalist Charles Waterton introduces an audio-visual tour of local wildlife and history. There are extensive walks around Anglers Lake and Haw Park woodlands. You can even have a meal or a coffee break at Waterton's home, now the Waterton Park Hotel, a Georgian mansion on an island in the lake at Walton Park, where he created the world's first nature reserve (now a golf course).

---

❻ Take the path across an open field towards the corner of Garden Plantation. The ruins of a gate lodge and a row of yew trees suggest that this was once a grander entrance to the old Chevet estate, a wider track than the present footpath.

❼ *Shorter route*: 20 yards into the plantation take the left-hand track at the crossroads of trackways, head over the bridge and up the slope, back towards the railway. There is oak, birch and bracken on the left of the path, Corsican pine and larch, planted for pit props, on the right. Corsican pine was introduced in 1799; it has long, yellowish-green needles which are sometimes twisted.

*Longer route*: at the crossroads of tracks continue straight on; after 300 yards look for a footpath down to your left, which leads to Newmillerdam lake. Turn right to follow the lakeside path in a clockwise direction. Newmillerdam village offers two pubs and a café (see *Food and Drink*). Continue the clockwise circuit of the lake out to the A62, left along the dam head, left again past the car park until, back at the headwaters of the lake, you reach a footbridge over Bushcliff Beck. Don't cross the bridge but continue in the direction you are heading for 400 yards, then, at a T-junction with a track, turn right and follow the track up to the old railway cutting.

❽ At the old cutting in the south-west corner of Newmillerdam Country Park turn left down the slope and follow the railway walk for ½ mile. The old track is shaded by birches. Below them grows wood avens, a pathside plant with hooked seeds which often hitch a ride on dogs.

❾ Some distance before you reach the bridge over the railway (the same one you passed on the way) look out for the track climbing up the slope amongst the birches to your left. This brings you back to the point where you turned down the slope towards the beck.

❿ Cross the bridge over the cutting and take the farm track back over open fields. After ½ mile, at the gate of Manor Farm (which has bright yellow doors on its barns), cross the wooden footbridge on the left and follow the footpath behind houses on your right. Turn right when you come out on Ingswell Avenue to return to Notton village green.

# HEATH

*Length: 3¼ miles*

| **Getting there**: Heath is just outside Wakefield, off the A655 Normanton road. | **Parking**: There is a car park on the heath opposite the Kings Arms. | **Map**: OS Pathfinder 692 Dewsbury and 703 Wakefield (South) (GR 356199). |
|---|---|---|

'Indeed I saw no Place so agreeable from the Time I set out, except Sir George Dalston's at Heath, esteemed one of the prettiest Villages in England, a mile from Wakefield', wrote the Rev John Mulso in a letter to Gilbert White in April 1761. It's a miracle that Heath, with the exception of the haunted Old Hall, has survived unscathed, with its stone-built mansions and humbler houses built around the

expanse of the green looking much as it did two hundred years ago. I can think of nowhere else quite like it. I'm surprised that it has never been used as the backdrop to a period drama.

Reg Dunn, who used to live in the flat in the stable block, remembered, as a boy, parties at the Hall, when the coachman would drop off the guests, see to their horses, then have a gathering of their own

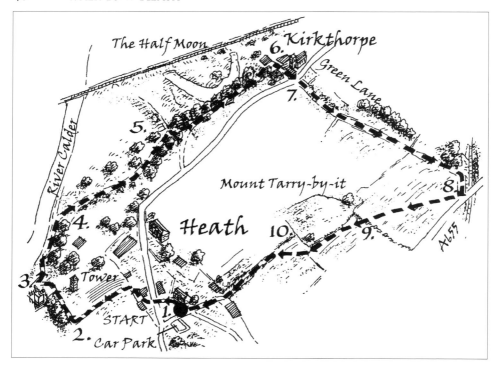

in the room above the stable. The Hall is now a ruin overlooking the valley.

Dame Mary Bolles, who lived at the Hall, was rumoured to have practised black magic (see Walk 7). Perhaps this was because she was the first person to have piped water pumped automatically up to her house. You will pass her water tower at the start of this walk. When she died in 1662 she asked for her room to be sealed. It

was opened 50 years later and her spirit is said to roam the common. A 'haunted door' from the Hall was once displayed in Wakefield Museum.

If you are walking in summer you'll see orchids in the valley. It's hard to believe that the attractive orchid woodland was, as recently as 30 years ago, featureless mud. The orchids, birches and oaks have colonised the fuel-ash beds of the old Wakefield power station. This walk takes in another remarkable village, Kirkthorpe, which has a church, almshouses and a set of stocks. The plain headstones of Benedictine nuns who fled the French Revolution lie at the east end of the church. They lived from 1811 to 1821 at Heath Old Hall.

---

**FOOD and DRINK**

The Kings Arms still has gaslight, a *real* open fire and oak-panelled walls. It offers bar meals lunchtimes and evenings, and there is a beer garden, conservatory and restaurant. Families are welcome and bookings are taken. Telephone: 01924 377527.

THE WALK

❶ With the Kings Arms behind you, head right and cross the road between the old school and the bus shelter. Turn right at the next small road ahead. At the corner of the large village green, diagonally opposite Heath Hall, take a short track on the left which after 20 yards becomes a footpath leading out over the fields. Dame Mary Bolles's water tower stands to your right.

❷ At the bottom of the field path turn right and follow a path with trees on your left.

❸ After passing an electric power compound, all that is left of Wakefield power station, the footpath comes out at a short stretch of concrete roadway. Turn right and follow the right-hand path, a permissive footpath over former fly-ash lagoons, now managed for their conservation value by Wakefield Metropolitan District Council.

❹ After 300-400 yards you'll have the River Calder on your left; take the path on the right where railway sleepers cross a small ditch. In a short while take a right fork again, so that you keep most of the open land to your left.

❺ In ½ mile, as you climb up the embankment, it is easiest to turn right to find a gentle slope back down to the path directly ahead. Follow this gently sloping path up through the wood. After 100 yards it is joined by a footpath from Heath on the right. The Half Moon, a cut-off meander of the Calder, and an old stone boathouse lie down the slope to your left. Continue onwards to Kirkthorpe.

❻ When you emerge at a metal gate at Kirkthorpe turn right up Half Moon Lane, past a foundation stone laid by Canon John Sharp MA on St James Day, 1899. At the top of this lane there are stocks by the almshouses on your right. Kirkthorpe church is on the left.

❼ Cross the road and take the public bridleway, Green Lane, ahead.

❽ When you reach the end of Green Lane at the A655, next to a railway cutting on your left, turn right to cross the large field diagonally, heading towards the left-hand side of Mount Tarry-by-it.

❾ Pass through the hawthorn hedge at a marker, crossing a small wooden bridge. Again head diagonally right at an angle of 45 degrees across this field, then follow the stone wall on your right.

❿ A kissing-gate takes you out of this field and again the path crosses diagonally to a kissing-gate in a hawthorn hedge. Go through it and follow the hedged path back to the village (there are traces of strip cultivation on the right), then turn right to return to the Kings Arms.

*Dame Mary Bolles's water tower.*

# WEST BRETTON

*Length: 5 or 3½ miles*

| **Getting there**: Bretton lies on the A637, 1 mile west of junction 38 of the M1. | **Parking**: Park in Bretton Country Park car park, on the A637 near junction 38 of the M1. | **Map**: OS Pathfinder 703 Wakefield (South) (GR 295125). |
|---|---|---|

Bretton's award-winning pie shop is a mecca for pork pie appreciation society members everywhere. Thankfully, for the sake of our waistlines, the village is blessed with excellent walking country. There's historic parkland around Bretton Hall (now a college), extensive woods and plantations, and a glimpse of the Yorkshire Wildlife Trust Bretton Lakes nature reserve. It's wonderful to see the herons perched in their tree-top nests on the islands. This is one of Yorkshire's wildlife spectaculars, made all the more special by its parkland setting.

The landscape garden, of which Bretton Country Park is a superb example, was one of England's great innovations in art and it has been copied all over the world. Out went fussiness, follies and formality, straight lines and statues. Designers such as

'Capability' Brown, who worked here, enlarged lakes and extended woodland to give a relaxed, natural feel to the landscape. Today you can see some of Henry Moore's powerful sculptures at the focus of the vistas in the wilder parts of the park. As you walk, decide for yourself whether their inclusion is in keeping with the aims of the Park's original designers. But enough of art criticism; just enjoy a landscape that shows what can be done when man and nature work together.

## FOOD and DRINK

'A clear and acclaimed winner...a pie of near mystical appeal', 'The taste – a dream. Incredibly meaty with super seasoning'. Hector Ellis started making his award-winning pork pies in Bretton back in 1953, but pies have been made on the premises at the little butcher's shop since the 1920s. Now's your chance to find out why the *Barnsley Chronicle* and Ripponden's Pork Pie Appreciation Society gave this pie the ultimate accolade of five stars. The Black Bull at Midgley a mile to the west of Bretton on the A637, is a spacious Brewer's Fayre house with a varied menu. Telephone: 01924 830260. The Old Post Office by the motorway junction at Haigh also serves meals. The Bothy Café, hidden away in the Sculpture Park, enjoys a panorama of the Dearne valley and serves coffees and teas, interesting lunches and tempting gateaux. It is open daily, 11 am - 5 pm.

## THE WALK

❶ Go through the gates by the information centre and head across the Park towards Bretton Hall. Pass a stone bridge and continue with the River Dearne on your left. Amongst the Canada geese look out for a few barnacle geese, which are smaller, with white faces. Take the gate in the bottom left-hand corner to enter Bretton Sculpture Park.

❷ Cross the parkland ahead, beneath a magnificent beech and cedar, then, when you've got to the end of the stone terrace of Bretton Hall, turn right up the gentle slope and head through the sculpture displays towards the camellia house. Follow the metalled track to the left of the camellia house (or alternatively, look for the access trail hidden amongst the trees to your left) and make your way up through the sculpture park car park to the conservatory which houses the sculpture park information centre. Continue up the drive

and, at the entrance lodge, follow the road to Bretton village. The old wall has clumps of grey lichen and stonecrop growing on it. Look out for the 'model' dairy and the old well on your left.

❸ When you reach the war memorial at the main road, turn left. If you want to sample a Hector Ellis pork pie, or visit the village store, take the next turn on the right; otherwise follow the main road out of the village. The long terrace of houses on your right was built using locally made brick.

❹ A few hundred yards after leaving the village, as you near the crest of the hill, take the forest track on your left, cross the wooden style and follow the track, which is a public footpath, into the woods. A clay pit on the site of Wakefield Naturalists' Society's Brickyard Plantation nature reserve was the source of much of the old brickwork in Bretton.

❺ At the crossroads of forest tracks take the footpath to the left, currently marked by an old wooden fingerpost 'To Bretton Park'. The track to Bentley Grange that continues ahead was once a main road but was superseded by a turnpike.

❻ Continue through the iron gates into open parkland, following the track ahead. The view opens up to show, on a clear day, a wind farm, Clayton West, the tops of the Pennines, the tower of Hoyland church amongst the trees of Hoyland Bank, Holme Moss and Emley Moor television masts with the valley of the River Dearne below. Ahead there's Barnsley on the skyline.

❼ On leaving the pasture at a gate turn right on the bridleway that skirts the western side of Bretton Sculpture Park. (For a short cut, return the way you came.) Pass through a galvanised gate and continue down the slope, with playing fields to your left and a row of poplars to your right, towards Bretton lakes. Go through the iron gates by the copper beech and lightning-struck sweet chestnut to cross the River Dearne and Cascade Bridge (actually a dam head between the upper and lower Bretton lakes).

❽ Leave the parkland by the iron gate and take the track up the slope ahead.

❾ In 500 yards, on reaching a stile on your right, turn sharp left on the footpath across open fields, towards a clump of trees in the dip. Continue over a stile, following red trail markers. At the cutting in the hillside, which was made to allow access during the upgrading of Bretton lakes dam, take the path up the right-hand embankment, marked with a red trail post.

❿ Climb up the ridge of Oxley Bank, which is a sandstone scarp. The path becomes stonier and the vegetation changes to wiry, wavy hair-grass and heath bedstraw on the thinner, drier soil.

⓫ At the top corner of Oxley Bank Wood, cross two stiles to continue along the field-edge path, marked with blue posts. Continue with the wood on your left, towards the drone of traffic on the M1,

*Bretton Hall* (courtesy of Roger Gaynor).

until the path turns right at the bottom of the field, to follow the fence.

**⑫** At the gate on the left, cross the stile and follow the field track which skirts the wood on your right. Continue with the drystone wall (which has an old stone trough built into it) on your right.

**⑬** At the stone barns, leave the field by the gate, continue ahead, then turn left when you come out on the metalled road.

**⑭** At the end of the lane turn left at the side of the short length of dual-carriageway,

**PLACES of INTEREST**

**Cannon Hall**, Cawthorne, near Barnsley, is another of the area's great parks. The Hall is now a museum featuring period rooms, regimental and mining history. There is a café and a children's farm in the grounds (tel: 01226 790427). The centrepiece of **Worsbrough Country Park**, two junctions down the motorway from Bretton near Barnsley, is a fully working watermill and its mill dam .

and follow the pavement, and old stretch of road, back to the gate lodge of the Country Park.

Bretton Lake from
the Cascade Bridge

# TONG

*Length: 3½ miles*

| **Getting there**: Tong lies south of Pudsey, on a minor road, Tong Lane, between Leeds and Bradford. | **Parking**: There are a few spaces opposite the church. | **Map**: OS Pathfinder 683 Leeds (GR 222206). |
|---|---|---|

Tong sits on its hilltop surrounded by fields, woods, valleys and, beyond them, a ring of towns and cities. Tong Hall, now a very desirable business address, was built in 1702 by Sir George Tempest and features carving by Grinling Gibbons. Near the entrance to the Hall, at the opposite end of the small green in front of the 18th-century church of St James, stands the Lantern House, a stone building with mullioned windows, dated 1615. It was once an inn, the lantern a guiding light for travellers. Don't miss the Edward VI postbox across the road.

Arthur Mee's *West Riding*, first published in 1941, describes a smithy next to the 1840s lion-headed village pump: 'We found the smith hard at work. One of seven generations to make horseshoes on the anvil here, he told us that his ancestors had shod horses in the Civil War.' There is a small pinfold, where stray animals were impounded, nearby.

Tong hasn't been swamped by commuter estates. This walk starts by leaving the main street and goes straight into working countryside – through the yard of a dairy and out among the cows. It follows a section of the Leeds Country Way through the woods and fields alongside Tong Beck and Pudsey Beck.

Towards the end of the walk, overlooking the golf course, there's the Moravian community of Fulneck. The Moravian Brethren, a Christian Protestant sect, were driven out of Bohemia in 1722 and took refuge in Germany, North America and England.

The Walk

❶ Walking away from the Greyhound towards Leeds, pass the end of Keeper Lane on your left and Hill Green Court on your right. Then cross the road and take the public footpath, through a small wooden gate, down the far side of a white house.

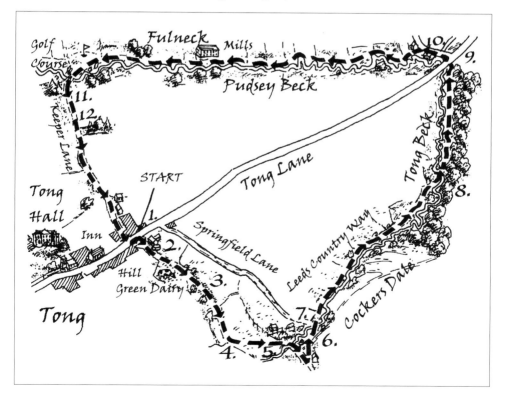

**❷** Pass through the yard of Hill Green Dairy, keeping the buildings and a slurry tank on your left. Cross a concrete yard and go through a metal gate onto a farm track. After you have crossed a narrow plot of land, another metal gate takes you out onto pastures.

**❸** Continue ahead downhill, keeping the field boundary, soon marked by a shallow ditch and a sprinkling of oak trees, about 20 yards on your left. Drighlington church stands across the valley to your right, behind a golf course.

**❹** In 500 yards, after descending a banking, you reach the field adjacent to the wood in the valley bottom. You should now head 45 degrees to your left, towards a stile in the bottom left-hand corner of the field at the edge of the wood.

**❺** Cross the wooden stile into the wood, turn right along a track and cross a stone bridge. Pass a pumping station on your left then, after passing through a kissing-gate next to what were the gates to a sewage works, turn sharp left onto a bridleway.

**❻** After 50 yards ignore a stile on your right by a metal gate which would take you along the top edge of Cockers Dale Wood and continue on the footpath ahead (part of the Leeds Country Way).

**❼** Cross the stream, then take the stile on the right where a footpath comes in from the left (Springfield Lane). Continue down

*Crocker's Dale.*

the valley with the stream on your right. Follow the path for ½ mile until, five stiles later, after passing a stone-lined spring on the left and going over a stretch of stone causeway across open scrubby land, the path goes through a stile by a stone gatepost, under trees and, after 20 yards, turns down towards the stream.

Village pump, Tong

❽ Cross the stream at a stile and a footbridge. Turn left and follow the path with the stream on your left for another ¼ mile.

❾ A kissing-gate between stone gateposts brings you out onto Tong Lane. Cross and take Roker Lane opposite into the Borough of Pudsey.

❿ In 100 yards, immediately after passing the mills, take the footpath on the left, again part of the Leeds Country Way. Follow this for a mile through the meadows, keeping within 50 or 60 yards of Pudsey Beck on the left. This stretch of footpath has recently been restored after pipe-laying by Yorkshire Water. The path keeps close to the stream as it passes mills, and a wood on the right then emerges at the lower edge of Fulneck Golf Course.

⓫ As you follow the path along the edge of the course, two footpaths come down across from Fulneck to the right. Just before you reach the second of these, turn left across the stream over the first of two footbridges.

⓬ The path soon starts to climb through the trees, with a drystone wall on the right. After 600 yards' climbing it comes out at the end of Keeper Lane. Follow this back to the start of the walk.

# HARTSHEAD

*Length: 2½ miles*

**Getting there**: Hartshead lies on a minor road between Brighouse and Roberttown.

**Parking**:There is a little on-road parking; alternatively, start at the Three Nuns at Mirfield, where there is on-road parking on the A644 opposite the pub.

**Map**: OS Pathfinder 691 Halifax (GR 185226).

If your experience of Hartshead is whizzing, or crawling, past the Hartshead Moor Services on the M62, you've missed out on a village with a fascinating history, surrounded by rolling countryside with views out over Calderdale.

The Rev Patrick Brontë was minister here from 1810 to 1815 and his eldest daughters were born locally. Charlotte attended Roe Head School and later taught there. Her novel *Shirley* is set in the area. You don't pass near to the school on this walk but as you reach the New Inn you'll see it down in the valley to your right. From 1960 to 1984 Roe Head was a seminary for missionary priests. Now it is a school for children with special needs. Hartshead church lies ¼ mile from the village, beyond

---

**FOOD and DRINK**

The Gray Ox, which was originally attached to a farm, selling milk and eggs as well as beer, is an inn which still always uses fresh ingredients in its imaginative meals, serving lunch from 12 noon to 2.30 pm and evening meals from 6 to 9.30 pm, with traditional Sunday lunch from 12 noon to 8.30 pm. There's an extensive à la carte menu (13 starters, 20 main courses) which includes plenty of seafood. Telephone: 01274 872845. The New Inn at the other end of the village serves traditional ales and lagers and bar meals. The Three Nuns, by the A62 at Mirfield, is a Big Steak Pub, open all day. The present building dates from 1939, replacing the original inn which had stood here since 1497. Finally, this is your only chance on one of these walks to sample the 'Early Starter' at the Little Chef.

---

the Gray Ox.

In 1812 a band of masked Luddites smashed machines being carted over Hartshead Moor. In the following year, after an attack on Rawfolds Mill, Luddites were hanged at York. A very different workers' group, the Chartists, were also active here; in 1842 a crowd of 250,000 attended a meeting on Peep Green at the north end of the village, and were addressed by firebrand orator Feargus O'Connor.

The Three Nuns Inn is a reminder of Kirklees Priory which stood nearby. Robin Hood is supposed to have died in its gatehouse, which still stands; he was bled to death by his cousin the prioress. He shot an arrow from the window and asked to be buried where the arrow fell, 660 yards away. In the 19th century railings were erected around the grave because chippings from the tombstone were reputed to cure toothache. You can't visit the grave today, but the inscription reads:

*Hear underneath dis laitl stean*
*Laz robert earl of Huntingtun*

*Ne'er arcir ver az hie sa geud*
*An pipl kauld im robin heud*
*Sick utlawz az hi an iz men*
*Vil england nivr si agen*
Obiit 24 Kal: Dekembris 1247

(My acknowledgements to Margaret M. Wood and her fascinating book *Hartshead & District in Times Past*. Every village should have a book like it.)

THE WALK

❶ At the Hartshead crossroads, or 'lane ends', with Hartshead Lane on your left and School Lane on your right, walk up Peep Green Road ahead. In 200 yards, at the brow of the hill, take the footpath over the worn stone stile on your left, immediately after a stone house. This path goes down between fields to emerge on Hartshead Lane 100 yards from the Gray Ox on your right.

❷ Take the footpath to the Three Nuns, almost opposite to the right. For the next ¼ mile this footpath takes you south with Almondbury Hill and the chimneys of Huddersfield ahead in the distance. Follow the right-hand boundary down the first field, then swing left with the path to follow the left-hand boundary of the next field. Cross a railway-sleeper bridge over a ditch, go straight across the next field and cross a field boundary of willows and oaks by a yellow chevron marker post. The path goes at 45 degrees to the right towards a stile in the bottom right-hand corner of the next field. Kirklees Hall is in the valley on your right.

❸ After crossing the stile take the track ahead, again signposted to the Three Nuns. The track runs between wire fences and

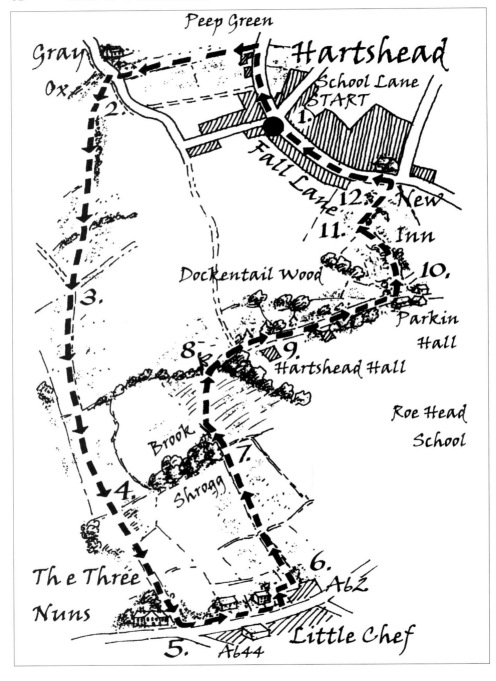

goes down into a dip with willows and planted poplars on the right. Ignore the footpath to Hartshead Hall on the left and continue on the track.

❹ At the end of the track cross a wooden stile next to a metal gate, signed 'Kirklees Way', and head across the field towards the Three Nuns. A similar stile takes you onto a track which brings you out at the side of the A62 with the Three Nuns on your right. (The Dumb Steeple, where the Luddites used to meet, stands by the roundabout 400 yards to your left.)

❺ Turn left and keep on this side of the A62. Continue for 250 yards, passing Nun Brook House and Yew Tree on your left and the Little Chef across the road on your right, then take the public footpath signed through an opening in the hawthorn hedge on your left, just after a square-fronted Georgian stone house.

❻ After 30 yards the path bends around a grassy area, then crosses a wooden stile ahead. A railway-sleeper footbridge takes you over a small stream, over another wooden stile and by a stone gatepost to follow paving stones along the left side of a sometimes muddy field.

❼ A stile takes you along the right-hand end of Brook Shrogg. In 30 yards, at the end of the drystone wall, the path heads diagonally right across the field towards a footpath sign in the top right corner, near the edge of a small wood.

*Brook Shrogg.*

❽ At the sign turn right along a green track with a wall and a small wood on your right.

❾ After 100 yards ignore the footpath on your left, continue on the track and go through a metal gate ahead. Follow the tarmac lane, passing a farm, Hartshead Hall, on your right (the Hall was demolished in 1959). After 100 yards a wooden gate takes you onto a track ahead. In another 250 yards a metal gate brings you out by the cottages of Parkin Hall (or Parkinhole). Luddite Cottage to the left of the lane ahead was the home of the Luddite-turned-traitor, William Hall. Don't go that far; turn immediately left on the footpath to Fall Lane.

❿ Go down 13 rough stone steps and a grassy slope. Continue between stone walls for 20 yards, through a stile between old stone posts and up the left-hand side of a hollow with a drystone-walled bank on your right. The path seems to follow the holloway most of the way, beneath hollies and oaks, then emerges at the top with a broken wall on the right.

⓫ Pass between two stone gateposts and turn right to follow a hedge line of old thorn trees on your right. Continue in the same direction across the next field towards the New Inn ahead.

⓬ Go through a stone stile and turn left along Fall Lane to the start of the walk.

Hartshead

# FARNLEY TYAS

*Length: 2½ miles*

| **Getting there**: Farnley Tyas lies south-east of Huddersfield between the A629 Penistone road and the A616 Holmfirth road. | **Parking**: On Butts Lane. There is a small parking area by Butts Terrace near the recreation ground. | **Map**: OS Pathfinder 702 Huddersfield and Marsden (GR 162125). |
|---|---|---|

Farnley Tyas sits surrounded by verdant pasture and deciduous woods. It's as if a valley from deepest Devon had been popped down right next to Huddersfield. The name itself conjures up the archetypal English village. Le Tyeis was the name of the Norman landlords. In 1923, when the landowner was the Earl of Dartmouth, there were 30 farms around the village but

these have now been combined into five.

The annual 'Sing-in' is a Whit Sunday procession through Molly Carr Woods, at their springtime best for bluebells and birdsong. You might think its origins would be lost in antiquity but it dates from 1900. Almondbury Hill, across the valley, has always been exploited as a prominent landmark. It was the site of an Iron Age

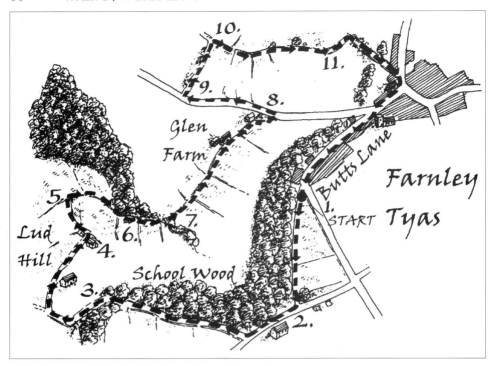

hill-fort; in 1588 a bonfire was lit there to celebrate the defeat of the Spanish Armada, and another at the time of the Huddersfield Riots (1820). The Victoria tower was built in 1898-9 to celebrate the Queen's diamond jubilee. The fundraisers hoped to top the 900-foot hill with a 100-foot tower, but funds ran out and it is only the tip of the flagpole that reaches 1,000 feet. On the latest OS maps the height is 'reduced' to a mere 270 metres, but from the top on a clear day you can still see York Minster. Don't worry, you don't have to climb Almondbury Hill today; this walk swings along the contours of the hills for much of the way, through woods and farmland.

---

**FOOD and DRINK**

The Golden Cock, which dates from the 17th century, has long had an outstanding reputation for out of the ordinary restaurant meals such as sole and spinach roulade with a watercress sauce, or fillet of beef with a Stilton soufflé. But you don't have to go cordon bleu; there's also a café bar with a blackboard menu and sandwiches are always available. Walkers are welcome. Telephone: 01484 66644.

---

THE WALK

❶ From Butts Lane, follow the right-hand side of the Dartmouth recreation ground, given to the village by the 6th earl in 1927, then take a wooden gate into a small field and continue, crossing stone steps by a metal gate. A short track brings you out on a lane.

**PLACES of INTEREST**

The **Tolson Memorial Museum**, Ravensknowle Park, Wakefield Road, Huddersfield, is strong on local history, from weaving to transport. Telephone: 01484 223830. I'm better at browsing and planning than actually completing my garden schemes so the **Pennine Garden Centre** at Shelley is an inspiration.

❷ Turn right along the lane and, in 200 yards, take the next track on the right, keeping School Wood on your right.

❸ Descend through a belt of woodland to emerge amongst meadows. Keep to the main track as it swings right to pass Ludhill Farm, ignoring the narrower footpath that goes down into the valley ahead.

❹ When this track ends by the next farmhouse turn left, then right on entering the field. Follow the right-hand side of this field down to the next steeply sloping field.

❺ Turn right along a path which follows the top of the slope close to the gritstone wall on your right. Ludhill Dike is down amongst the trees on your left.

❻ Keep on this path along the top of the wood and along the bottom edge of the next two fields, then follow it into the wood, cross the stream, and climb steps up through the wood.

❼ On emerging at the top end of the wood, follow the left-hand side of the next four fields, passing Glen Farm. As you get towards the road, the path makes a short detour to the right around an enclosure.

❽ Turn left down the road, keeping to the pavement on the right.

❾ In 250 yards, follow the footpath along the green lane to the right.

❿ When you come to the end of this path, turn right and follow the path along the left-hand side of the next four fields until you reach the end of a lane.

⓫ Follow this sometimes muddy lane back up to Farnley Tyas. At the road turn right to return, via the Golden Cock, to Butts Lane.

# DENBY DALE

*Length: 4 miles*

**Getting there**: Denby Dale lies on the A636. There are regular train and bus services.

**Parking**: There are two public car parks on the main street.

**Map**: OS Pathfinder 715 Barnsley (GR 227085).

No list of Yorkshire villages would be complete without Denby Dale, the Pie Village. The pie, of mammoth proportions, is the centrepiece of an occasional festival. The proceeds have been used to provide the village with its Pie Hall.

The village has retained its gritty, mill-town looks. The stone-built railway viaduct striding across the valley above the old stone terraces, pubs and mills gives Denby

Dale a strong visual identity. With its road and rail connections, the village is a good centre for exploring the woods and haymeadows of the surrounding dale. The Langsett Moors on the edge of the Peak District to the south are as close as the Holme Moss at the crest of the Pennines to the west.

There is a birding side to the village, which houses the RSPB regional office. If

**FOOD and DRINK**

The Dalesman on the main street offers food and a lively atmosphere. For more traditional surroundings try the Dunkirk on the road out of the village towards Upper Denby, which is recommended for its meals. Telephone: 01484 862646. Springfield Mills has a coffee shop and there is a sandwich bar near the viaduct.

you get a strange feeling that you are being watched don't worry, that's just the birders testing out the binoculars and telescopes at the 'In Focus' shop perched above the town by the station. Over 100 species of birds have been seen from the shop including great spotted woodpecker (coming to the bird feeder) and peregrine falcon. RSPB officer Tim Melling tells me that you'll still see plenty of linnets and yellowhammers on the local farmland, even though their numbers are down nationally. Other local birds include little owl, kingfisher, nuthatch, green woodpecker and various warblers.

This walk touches on three neighbouring villages: Upper Denby, set amongst Pennine haymeadows, Quaker Bottom, tucked away in a quiet corner, and Upper Cumberworth, further up the dale. There are sweeping views punctuated by deep, narrow, wooded cloughs. Stone walls, stone-step stiles, cobbles and causey stones give this walk true Pennine character.

THE WALK

❶ At the centre of Denby Dale, 400 yards east of the viaduct, turn south down Norman Road, passing Springfield Mills on your left. Cross the road and continue ahead up Trinity Drive, marked as a public footpath, towards the church, which has a foundation stone dated 1938.

❷ Go through a stone stile into the field ahead and continue uphill, ignoring a causey-stone path to your right. Leave the field by a stone stile, turn left along the road for just 30 yards, then cross into Broom Bank. Between the second and third houses on your right, take the footpath which passes under the railway embankment through an imposing stone arch.

❸ Cross a rustic stile and continue straight up the field, with a wire fence on your right. Enter Hagg Wood through a stone stile, turn left and follow the bridleway around the north-east corner of the wood. There is a long stretch of cobbles as the bridleway climbs through oaks, sycamores and foxgloves from pastures at the foot of the slope to haymeadows above.

❹ At a crossroads of footpaths continue on the lane ahead, pass the stone gateposts of a long driveway to your right, and take the next lane on your right. This runs alongside the gardens of the first row of houses of Upper Denby village, the first of them a large stone bungalow called Lemonacre.

❺ After the row of houses, ignore the footpath which enters the lane from the left, from the direction of Upper Denby church, and follow the lane around the corner to two metal gates. Cross the stone-step stile, the first of many, by the left-hand gate to enter the field on your left. Continue with a drystone wall on your right to the next set of stone steps in the far right-

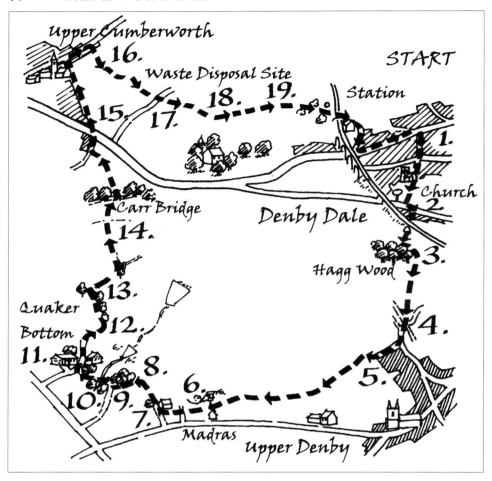

hand corner of this long field. The large stone farmhouse of Moist Holme is on your left.

❻ Repeat the process of crossing walls by stone steps and continuing with a drystone wall on your right until, after passing a small quarry on your right and a brick house (called Madras on older OS maps) with concrete stables on your left, you come out on a lane.

❼ At the lane turn left for just 10 yards and climb another step stile to cross the wall opposite. After crossing a small field, climb yet more stone steps to emerge near the end of a second lane, by a cast iron lamp-post. Turn right, through a metal gate, passing a large stone house on your right, and cross the wall ahead by a stone step under the spreading sycamore.

❽ Follow the wall on your left down

towards a copse. There is a small dam ahead. Take the first stone stile on your left, near the corner of the copse. Follow the wall of the copse on your right, then go through the metal gate.

❾ Cross to the flagstone stile and you come to two metal gates, side by side, at the end of a farm track. The right-hand gate is marked 'NO ENTRY! DANGER KEEP OUT'. Take the large stone-step stile between the gates, which leads to an open access area, in the hollow around the pond, where you are welcome to picnic (if you can avoid the thistles).

❿ Follow the causey stones down the left-hand side of this open access field into the steep little valley of Munchcliffe Beck. Go through a small wooden gate and down the 39 steps beneath the sycamores to cross the bridge over the beck. Emerge through the metal gate and climb the hill with the gardens of Quaker Bottom on your right. The path winds through a narrow stone passageway before emerging at the fine stone buildings of the settlement of Quaker Bottom, established in the 17th century. The Friends' Meeting House was constructed using techniques now used to build drystone walls.

⓫ Follow the cobbled lane through the settlement and continue, past the Meeting House and burial ground on your left, over a wooden stile by a metal gate to a grassy track which curves down-slope.

⓬ At the bottom of this field, just before you reach the metal gate and wooden stile, with the small dam now down in the dip on your right, turn left in front of the large

*Carr Bridge.*

---

**PLACES of INTEREST**

Some of Yorkshire's great little steam trains run on the **Kirklees Light Railway**, at Clayton West on the A636 Wakefield road. There's a children's play area, café and free parking. The railway is open every weekend and weekdays too between spring bank holiday and the end of August, as well as most school holidays. Telephone: 01484 865727.

---

holly and old ash to follow a belt of trees along the lower edge of the field. The footpath is not very obvious, but you want to finish up in the bottom right-hand corner of this field, where there are two drystone walls, about 15 yards apart, and leave by the stile in the corner.

⓭ Stone steps emerge onto an open slope. Set off down the hill but look for a path that veers left past three isolated oaks on the right and a fourth on the left. The slope levels out at the corner of a drystone wall; take the stone-step stile by the wooden gate on your left, heading north with Upper Cumberworth church ahead on the ridge.

⓮ Cross a further stile, with bench-like wooden steps, down four stone steps, and cross the field heading half-right to find a small gap in the wall opposite. Take the steep steps down amongst the trees to cross Carr Bridge, a wooden footbridge. Cross a lane and head up the roadside field, aiming slightly to the left, towards a bungalow with dormer windows, the third building back from the main road. On emerging in the lane turn right towards the main road.

⓯ Cross the A635 and take the public footpath signed up the lane opposite. This soon turns into a footpath running behind houses on the left with pastures to the right. On emerging near St Nicholas church, turn right and, before leaving the village, look for the footpath on your right, between numbers 58 and 60.

⓰ Follow the field boundary on your left for about 50 yards, then take the wooden stile through the hawthorn hedge. Keep more or less to the right side of the next field, cutting off a shallow corner to cross a stone stile. Follow the path which, after 30 or 40 yards, turns right around the angle of a drystone wall. A restored landscape, once a clay quarry but now a waste disposal site, appears on your left. Head towards a metal gate.

⓱ Use two stiles to cross the access road, then set off half-left across the next small field. Take the wooden stile out of this field and back towards the road a short way until a path takes you to the right along the edge of the waste disposal site, with wire fences on either side.

⓲ On entering the next field head half-left with Rockwood House down in the dip on your right and the waste disposal site on your left. Tall green methane ventilators echo the shape of Emley Moor mast in the distance.

⓳ Continuing with the site on your left you will eventually reach a gate at the end of a lane. Cross the fence near the large gatepost, a sawn-off telephone pole, and follow the lane down to Denby Dale station. From there follow the road down to the main street and the start of the walk.

# NEW MILL

*Length: 5 miles*

| Getting there: New Mill is on the A635,1½ miles west of Holmfirth. | Parking: Car park and toilets on the Holmfirth road, opposite the turn to Totties and Scholes, near the chimney of Moorbrook Mills. | Map: OS Pathfinder 714 Holmfirth (GR 162089). |
| --- | --- | --- |

Viewers of the long-running television comedy *Last of the Summer Wine* will find parts of this walk familiar. New Mill is much as Holmfirth was before it became so celebrated, with its regular coach tours and its Wrinkled Stocking Café. As you climb to New Mill's church, you'll pass stone-built weavers' cottages, with long rows of mullioned windows to give extra light on the upper storey. The rugged, individual character of the village is matched by the moorland edge setting with deep valleys between gritstone edges.

The Maythorne cross which has been restored and re-erected by the village library dates from the early 15th century. Opposite stands a hunting lodge, dated 1773, now part of the White Hart. In

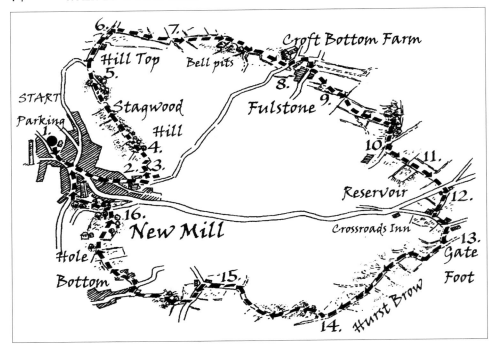

addition to two mill chimneys the village has an old brewery, sadly no longer brewing.

You're right on the edge of the outcrop of millstone grit which underlies the South Pennine moors. On the flanks of the moors lie the coal measures. Just before you reach the hamlet of Fulstone you'll see a couple of bell pits which were probably dug more than 200 years ago to win coal from a seam not far beneath the surface. Most of the old field pattern has survived around Fulstone. The long, narrow strips of fields suggest the enclosure of a medieval open field.

Yes, this walk does involve some climbing, especially at the beginning, but after that there are stretches, notably along Hurst Brow, when you can stride out along the crest of the ridge and enjoy the panorama spread out below.

## THE WALK

❶ Turn left out of the car park and at the crossroads take the Barnsley and Wakefield A635 road ahead up the hill. After 50 yards turn left up Sude Hill.

❷ As you approach the churchyard take Fulstone Hall Lane which forks left, passing the church on your right.

❸ Opposite the last house, Stony Gables, turn left down a driveway and cross an old mill yard.

Take the grassy path opposite, then cross the stile, turn right and follow the right-hand side of the field, passing beneath power lines. After following a gritstone wall around the corner of the field you enter a small oak-wood.

**❹** Cross a wooden stile over a barbed wire fence, then cross open hillside, following a wire fence on your left. The footpath goes along the edge of the woodland to the right of a broken wall and crosses a stone stile by some holly bushes. Continue on a raised path between hollies on your right and the top of the wall on your left.

**❺** When the path joins a track coming in from the right, follow it onwards, to your left. After 40 or 50 yards a metal gate brings you out on a sharp bend on a narrow road. Turn right up the hill.

**❻** After passing the entrance to Hilltop Farm on your right, and a footpath on your left, take the footpath to the right across a broken wall, a rushy area and over a wooden stile into a pasture.

Follow the stone wall on your right to the end of this field, ignoring a footpath to the right. Cross the stile in the far right-hand corner, then look for the next stile ahead, by a holly bush between a couple of

sycamore trees.

**❼** Cross this stile then, in the next field, follow the wall on your left. Another stone stile takes you through an angled wall. Again keep to the wall on your left. Pass the remains of two old bell pits. At the second pit take a step stile over a wall by a metal gate and head at an angle of 45 degrees towards the corner of a wall on your right. Then continue over the field, keeping the wall on your right, towards a big beech tree to the right of Croft Bottom Farm.

**❽** Emerging at a gap in the wall by two beech trees at the hamlet of Fulstone, turn left along the narrow road. Before you reach the telephone box turn right off Fulstone Hall Lane onto White Ley Bank. Ignore the first public footpath on your left after 20 yards, then, after another 10 or 20 yards, take a turning on your left between Fulstone Croft and Moor View Barn.

Enter the field by a metal gate to the right of a garage. Cross the field diagonally towards a stile on your right. The footpath differs from that shown on the OS map, so please follow any waymarks.

**❾** In the next long, narrow field, head towards the step-ladder stile in the bottom right-hand corner.

From the stile, head diagonally right again but ignore the next stile in the wall on the right. Head up the slope to the right-hand corner to find a little step-ladder stile which takes you up the wall into the strip of woodland. Follow the path through the trees to your right, crossing a broken wall.

**❿** When you come out at the stile at the

## PLACES of INTEREST

**Holmfirth**, besides the *Summer Wine* connections, is the home of **Bamforth's**, publishers of saucy postcards since Edwardian days. They also made pioneering one-reelers in the early days of silent film, with comedies and thrilling little adventures, featuring fires, chases, cute kids and even canine co-stars. The postcard museum closed in 1977 but some of the postcards are displayed in the foyer of the library. Telephone: 01484 222430. Another local legend is Ashley Jackson, who has his **Artist's Shop** in the town.

top corner of the wood, turn right along the path for about 20 yards, then take a stone stile on your left along a footpath waymarked as part of the Kirklees Way.

**⓫** When the next stile brings you to the corner of a neat wall around Shepley service reservoir, the main A635 road comes into view. On reaching the road, take the passageway between the houses opposite.

**⓬** Turn right along the next quiet road and follow it 200 yards to the next T-junction. Turn left uphill. The meadow opposite is rich in wild flowers in early summer. (If you're ready for a break, you could call in at the Crossroads Hotel, just down the hill to your right.)

As the road swings left turn right along a track up the hill.

**⓭** After 300 yards, at a T-junction of tracks, turn right. After 50 yards ignore the footpath down to Upper Holme Farm on your right and, for the time being, keep on

*The White Hart pub, with the 15th-century Maythorne Cross in the foreground.*

the Kirklees Way, which becomes a metalled track.

❹ At a crossroads of lanes, leave the Kirklees Way and turn right down the hill at a small quarry. Head down this holloway lane, which becomes a metalled road.

❺ On arriving at two bungalows on your right and a row of cottages ahead, turn left along a narrow road.

After 150 yards take the footpath on your right down a path which, after a stone-step stile, follows a narrow gully, crossing railway-sleeper bridges.

On reaching the road at Hole Bottom turn right, uphill, and take the first road on your left after 30 yards. Follow this cul-de-sac round to the left, passing an old pump and ending up at a stone stile that leads into a field. One of the houses is dated IK 1742.

Walk through the field with a wall on your left, cross a wall line and carry on to pass through a metal kissing-gate by a line of large oaks. Then follow causey stones to a gate, under a small-leaved lime, which takes you down stone steps to a road.

❻ Look for the gap opposite and slightly to the left and follow a path down a wooded bank. A lane brings you out at the square chimney of Glendale Mills. Turn right to return to the crossroads and the start of the walk. You pass the old brewery on your right.

# MARSDEN

*Length: 4¼ miles*

| **Getting there**: Marsden lies on the A62 Manchester road and has its own station on the Manchester to Huddersfield line. | **Parking**: Plenty of parking in the village, also a car park at Tunnel End Visitor Centre. | **Map**: OS Pathfinder 702 Huddersfield and Marsden and Outdoor Leisure 21 South Pennines (GR 047118). |
| --- | --- | --- |

Marsden has kept the atmosphere of a 'real' northern town as described in the novels of Stan Barstow. It is a little mill town but on such a small scale, and with such inviting rambles around it, that it merits a place in this book. The high street, dominated by the town's Mechanics' Institute, still has far more local businesses than national franchises. The bird's eye

view of the town and its mill from the end of the walk is like a Lowry painting.

'Enoch meks 'em! Enoch breks 'em!' chanted the Luddites as they smashed shearing frames with a trusty sledge hammer. The hammer (which can be seen in Tolson Museum, Huddersfield) was named after Enoch Taylor (1780-1837) of Marsden, engineer and iron founder, who

**FOOD and DRINK**

On a weekend, before (or even after) your walk, try breakfast at the Swan, where it is served from 9 to 11 am. The National Trust's summer solstice sunrise walk (telephone: 01484 847016) finishes here for breakfast at 6.30 am! Bistro lunches are served from 12 noon to 2 pm on weekdays, and at weekends from 12 noon to 4 pm. This isn't a fast-food establishment; everything is made on the premises and cooked fresh to order. We particularly appreciated the comfortable no-smoking dining room. Telephone: 01484 844308. Further along the main street there's the Village Bakery bistro and coffee lounge, a wholefood café, the Shakespeare public house, the New Inn, with hot and cold food and, up by the station, the Railway Inn with snug, games room and lounge. The Hey Green, beyond Tunnel End, is a three-star, four-crown restaurant and country house hotel.

is buried on the green by St Bartholomew's parish church. The stocks nearby are a relic of medieval Marsden.

Old Mount Road, met on the walk, was part of the turnpike laid out by Blind Jack of Knaresborough across the moors in 1759. He used bundles of heather as the base of the road over boggy ground. But his was not the first trans-Pennine crossing; parts of a Roman road and a medieval packhorse route have been excavated on the south slopes of Pule Hill.

The engineer Thomas Telford worked on the Standedge Canal tunnel, which opened in 1811. On 4th April the previous year the 'Black Flood' swept through the town when Swellands reservoir burst. The body of one of the casualties was washed away to Huddersfield. Another casualty in that year was William Horsfall, a local mill-owner, who was shot by a group of Luddites while riding home from the cloth markets in Huddersfield. He had called in soldiers and erected barricades to protect

his mill. Later, railway tunnels ran parallel to the canal. Holidaymakers on their way to Manchester airport's new station still benefit from the toil of Victorian navvies.

Walking boots are recommended as this walk follows a section of the Standedge Trail, part of which is not a public footpath, over open moorland. There is a small ford across the Redbrook. The bed of the stream is rocky and, when we tried it, the water did not reach the top of my boots, but it may be impassable at times. Having said that, this is a good introduction to moorland walking as the route doesn't stray too far from landmarks such as the A62.

THE WALK

❶ From the station follow the Huddersfield Narrow Canal towpath walk, part of the Kirklees Way, west to Tunnel End.

❷ Cross the bridge over the canal at Tunnel End, turn right and follow the road up the hill towards Tunnel End Inn. Ignoring the sharp left turn, turn left on Waters Road.

❸ About 100 yards after passing the entrance to Hey Green Hotel take the footpath that forks left to 'Willy Kay Clough'. This follows the river bank and then crosses a packhorse bridge onto the edge of Marsden Moor.

This Pennine moorland is part of the South Pennines Moors Site of Special Scientific Interest. The birds that live here include curlew, golden plover, peregrine and merlin. Please ensure that they have the peace they need to raise their young successfully.

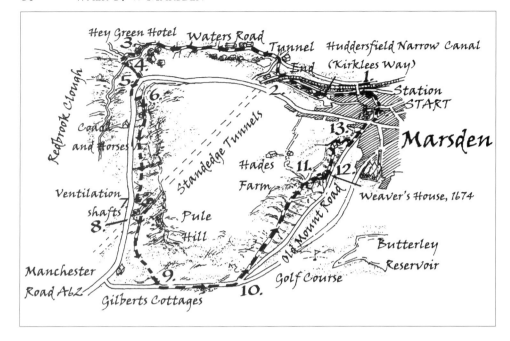

❹ After crossing the packhorse bridge, bear left and look for a way across the stream. This is the Redbrook; the rusty iron deposits on the stream bed can be slippery. Go through a narrow gate to follow the path between drystone walls up the hill.

❺ At the A62 Manchester road turn right. After 200 yards cross the road and take the footpath up five railway-sleeper steps. Cross the stile, go up the right-hand side of a boulder-strewn field and cross a step-ladder stile to come out on a narrow grassy track.

❻ Turn right behind the buildings of Lower Owlers Farm and follow this path for ½ mile parallel to the road down on your right. In places it is not much more than a sheep track. It includes a boggy slope with duckboards opposite the Coach and Horses,

then continues with a drystone wall on the right. You pass through one stile to leave Marsden Moor and, in 200 yards, a second stile to come back onto it.

❼ When you reach an old spoil mound, between two tunnel shafts, take the path that goes up to the left. Turn right when you reach the track that runs alongside the tunnel shafts, again parallel to the road below.

❽ When you get near the lower tunnel shaft, fork left along a narrow grassy path with power lines on your right. You soon cross the incline from the disused Pule Edge quarry to the road then, after ¼ mile, the path begins to turn away from the road some distance behind Gilbert Cottages (built to house navvies) and the second of

### PLACES of INTEREST

For more information on the history, and natural history, of the area **Tunnel End Visitor Centre** is open at weekends. Telephone: 01484 846062. **Huddersfield** and **Holmfirth**, mentioned in previous chapters, are nearby. At the other side of the moor, 5 miles along the A62, there are the Pennine villages of **Delph** and **Dobcross** with weavers' cottages, craft shops and country pubs. **Castleshaw Roman Fort** stands above Delph, its reconstructed banks and ditches guarding the Roman road from Chester to York.

three inns along this stretch of the A62. A stone slab takes you across a gully.

**❾** At the road turn left. After ¼ mile, as you pass an old quarry track on your left, take a look at the little bridge down in the dip to the right, part of Blind Jack's 1759 turnpike road.

**❿** After another 300 yards, take the next road on your left, Old Mount Road, then immediately fork left on the track to Hades Farm, over National Trust land. There is a panorama of the golf course and Butterley reservoir down to the right and Marsden's mills ahead.

**⓫** After ½ mile, as the track curves left by mounds of quarry waste, go down to the right to a gate and stile in the corner of the wall and descend, with great care, a rushy path, picking your way over stones that have fallen from the gritstone walls on either side. This lasts only 150 yards, then you come out on a green lane with a weaver's cottage, dated 1674, on your left.

**⓬** Turn left and follow the grassy path along the hillside parallel to Old Mount Road below. At Manor House Farm, a rendered house with stone mullions, turn right and continue right again around the buildings to follow the driveway to the farm, a hairpin bend, down to Old Mount Road.

**⓭** Turn left, then cross the A62 to Towngate ahead. Pass the church on your left to return to Station Road, the start of the walk.

# RIPPONDEN

*Length: 4¼ miles*

| **Getting there**: Ripponden lies 5 miles from junction 22 of the M62 on the A672 Halifax road. | **Parking**: There is a free car park by the church and another across the river, behind the Conservative Club on Royd Lane. | **Map**: OS Outdoor Leisure 21 South Pennines (GR 041198). |
|---|---|---|

Ripponden has long been an important crossroads and a staging post for packhorse teams working the trans-Pennine trails. The village is centred around an ancient packhorse bridge by the 15th-century church of St Bartholomew and an equally ancient inn, probably the oldest in Yorkshire.

On the first Sunday in September a rushbearing procession makes its way through Ripponden, amid mummers' plays and Morris dancing, brass bands, barbecues and boat trips. The ceremony dates back to the 17th century, when fresh rushes were cut to strew on the stone floors of local churches. The rushes are elaborately stacked 16 feet high on the cart, which is pulled by 60 local men, wearing clogs, black trousers, white shirts and Panama hats. A village maid rides on top of the whole edifice. Appropriately, Rishworth, below the village, has an Anglo-Saxon name meaning 'homestead among the rushes'. Ripponden was 'Riburndene', possibly from the Anglo-Saxon '*hrife burn*' meaning 'fierce stream in a wooded valley'.

A railway walk takes you out of the village and you return by a riverside path. This walk follows a wooded valley to Rishworth, climbs to the edge of Pike End (on the cross-country route for the energetic pupils of Rishworth school), then turns down to Ryburn reservoir which has a picnic site and toilets. Rishworth New Mill (1868), now converted into apartments, had one of the world's largest waterwheels, weighing 70 tons, with a span of nearly 58 feet and a width of 12 feet.

## THE WALK

❶ From the church walk up Bridge End and turn left up Elland Road. After 100 yards take the public footpath to 'Ringstone Edge via Height Walk', up the old railway embankment on your right. Follow the railway walk as far as you can, squeezing through a stile in the wall ahead at the first bridge to follow the footpath to 'Quaker Lane and Riverside'.

❷ After nearly ½ mile the railway walk ends by a cast-iron footbridge. Climb down a wooden stepladder, then go round to cross the footbridge. The footpath climbs, turning right, parallel to the railway, for a while.

❸ After 50 yards turn right at a T-junction of paths. Follow this hillside path for 300 yards, then fork right downhill to follow a concrete track.

❹ At the bottom of the concrete ramp turn left on the track alongside the beck, and follow this up the valley. The track becomes a footpath as it passes to the left of a stone-built farmhouse. It then passes through woodland, crossing a small stream by a plank bridge. On emerging in a field, keep to the left, close to the trees, heading for Rishworth Mill ahead.

❺ Cross a wooden stile by an iron gate and turn right, then left, around the back of the pylon, towards Rishworth Mill. A stile takes you into the old mill yard, now a parking area. Turn right and make your way out of the car park towards the road.

❻ Head straight towards the main road along the old road, to come out opposite the left-hand end of a turning circle. Cross the road and take the footpath to 'Arkin Royd and Pike End' straight ahead.

❼ At the road turn right towards St John's church, Rishworth, but before you reach it, take the footpath on your left behind the houses of Godly opposite.

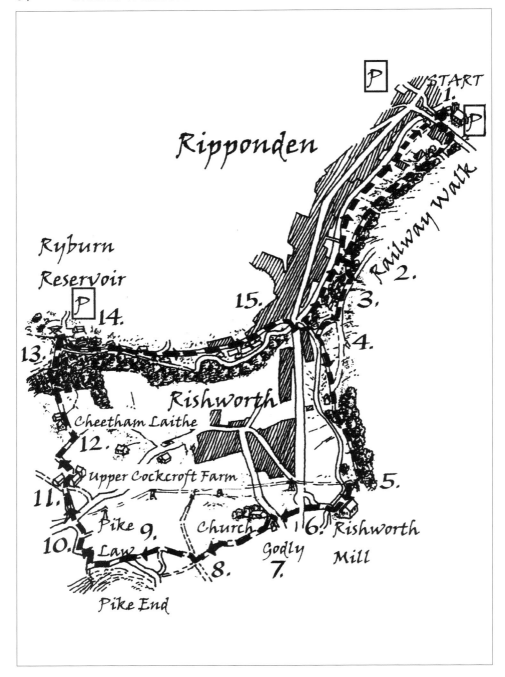

Ripponden

Railway Walk

START
1.

2.

3.

4.

Ryburn
Reservoir
14.

15.

5.

13.

Rishworth

Cheetham Laithe

12.

Upper Cockcroft Farm

11.

Pike    9.
10.  Law

Church    6.  Rishworth
Godly        Mill
8.    7.

Pike End

---

**PLACES of INTEREST**

**Eureka!** next to the station in Halifax was Britain's first interactive museum designed especially for children between three and 12 years. Winner of the English Tourist Board's Visitor Attraction of the Year, it has more than 400 larger than life exhibits designed to encourage children to use their imaginations and their senses. Telephone: 01422 330069.

---

**⑧** After climbing for 400 yards you reach a crossroads of footpaths. Turn right then, very shortly, left and follow the path up across the hillside for another 300 yards until you come out at a bend on a lane.

**⑨** Go ahead, right, along the lane and, in 200 yards at Pike Law at a sharp turn where a footpath connects with the road, continue with the road downhill to the right.

**⑩** After following the road downhill for another 200 yards you come to a T-junction. Take the footpath opposite.

**⑪** In 100 yards, after crossing another footpath, continue ahead then right, behind the buildings of Upper Cockcroft Farm.

**⑫** In another 200 yards continue ahead between two stone gateposts to Cheetham Laithe Farm. Pass the buildings on your left on your way down towards Ryburn reservoir, which is hidden amongst trees.

*Ryburn reservoir.*

**ⓑ** A small stile by an iron gate takes you into the wood. Turn right on reaching the reservoir path and follow it over the dam head to the picnic area and toilets. Ryburn and Baitings reservoirs were built between 1881 and 1956 to supply Wakefield with drinking water. The 100-foot high dam was built between 1925 and 1933, using a 1,015-foot aerial ropeway to carry materials to the site. There is a new permissive footpath on the north side of the reservoir.

**ⓓ** Take the 'Ripponden via Stones' footpath down from the north side of the dam head. Partway down the flights of stone steps look for a footpath branching off to the left over a wooden stile. The path emerges in front of a garage and continues downhill along a lane, down a cobbled slope, then onto a narrow road. Keep to the road, passing a row of cottages, until eventually you come out on the A672 Oldham road.

**ⓔ** Turn right over the bridge, then take the first left turn, in front of a mill, to follow the public footpath down Holme House Lane. Cross a smaller bridge and turn left for 'Ripponden via Riverside Path'. Stay on this side of the river to return to the start of the walk, finally crossing a playing field and passing through an archway under the Elland road.

# HEPTONSTALL

*Length: 5½ miles*

| **Getting there**: Heptonstall is a steep climb from Hebden Bridge (which has a station) on the A646 Halifax to Todmorden road. | **Parking**: There is a car park at the Hebden Bridge end of the village. | **Map**: OS Outdoor Leisure 21 South Pennines (GR 987281). |
|---|---|---|

With its narrow alleyways and cobbled streets, the hilltop village of Heptonstall strikes me as by far the most extraordinary I've visited. One grey overcast morning we climbed the steep alleys from the station – much the best, though not the easiest, way to approach Heptonstall. On Northgate, as we looked at the 18th-century couple carved over a door, a countryman strode by in authentic Cromwellian costume: a member of a Civil War re-enactment society. I felt that we were the ones who were out of place, in our off-the-peg anoraks.

In a little over 5 miles this walk takes you along two cloughs, as the deep, narrow wooded valleys are called, and up to as exhilarating a stretch of moorland as you

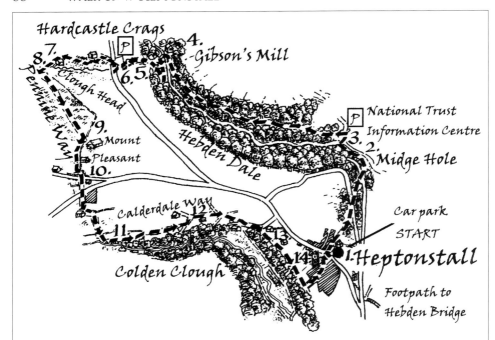

could wish to see. It's a chance to sample a bite-sized chunk of the challenging Pennine Way.

In the *Pennine Way Companion* Alfred Wainwright sketched an old stone footbridge over Colden Water. Commenting on the steep alleys of Hebden Bridge, he reckoned it was a wonder the town hadn't produced a supply of Everest climbers. He wrote of Hebden Dale, better known as Hardcastle Crags: 'this valley has long been known to Lancashire and Yorkshire people as an idyllic retreat... "The Switzerland of the North" it was named in older days, and excursion trains brought to Hebden Bridge station hundreds of visitors every summer weekend.'

We saw coal tit and treecreeper in the Hardcastle Crags woods, then heard red grouse up on the moor. Amongst the trees in the valley are domed mounds, meticulously constructed from pine needles – the nests of wood ants.

THE WALK

❶ From the car park, walk back to Heptonstall Road, turn right and then right again into Northgate by the Cross Inn.

(Look for the 18th-century equivalent of a wedding photograph carved above the lintel on your left, dated FHE 1736. A little further on, a lintel over an alleyway is inscribed IB 1578. This is the entrance to Whitehall Farm, originally Bentleys, home to a Heptonstall family that included Dr Richard Bentley (1662-1742), Master of Trinity College, Cambridge, said to be the most brilliant classical scholar of his age.

Heptonstall's octagonal Methodist church,
where Wesley often preached, is a little
further on, down to the right.)

Opposite the start of Northfield Terrace
and Northfield turn right down the grassy
footpath, to the right of Stocks Villas 1888,
signed 'Calderdale Way'. Follow this path
down into the valley for ½ mile, crossing
first a road and then a lane.

❷ At a T-junction with a riverside path
turn left on the footpath marked
'Calderdale Way to Hardcastle Crags'.

❸ After passing Midge Hole Working
Men's Club (visitors are welcome to the
Blue Pig bar), turn right over the stone
bridge. Ignore the small path immediately
over the bridge marked 'National Trust
Hardcastle Crags' and continue up the lane
for 70 yards, then turn sharp left at the
entrance to the National Trust car park and
information centre.

With the car park and information
centre on your right, go along the lane
ahead, ignoring paths down to the left and
the lane turning up to the right. Continue
through a barrier onto the main forest track

ahead which you follow for a mile.

❹ At Gibson's Mill turn left over the
bridge (or the stepping stones).

(As the information board will tell you,
Gibson's Mill was built in 1800 as a water-
powered cotton mill. It is named after the
founder, Abraham Gibson, who owned a
cotton-spinning business across the valley
at Greenwood Lee. In 1833 there were 22
workers here; the weekly pay for a man was
17 shillings, for a woman 6/6d and for a
child between 10 shillings and 12/6d. The
mill's five-horsepower waterwheel was
replaced in the 1860s by a steam engine.
Production ceased in the 1890s and until
1939 the mill was open to visitors to
Hardcastle Crags; it featured a dining
saloon, a roller skating rink and dance hall.

❺ Over the bridge turn left and take the
gently sloping track up the hill. After 200
yards, just past a small stone shelter and just
before a cobbled stretch starts, swing sharp
right on a path up through the wood.

After another 200 yards' climb you are
back above the mill; turn right up the hill
onto a track. There is a deep clough to your
right. A stone step stile by a metal gate
takes you out of the wood.

❻ After another gate the track emerges at
the road. Turn right past the National
Trust car park and, in less than 100 yards,
take the footpath on your left up a concrete
farm track and over a cattle grid towards
Clough House Farm.

The footpath avoids the farmyard; just
before the gate, turn left along the field-
edge path and go through two metal gates,
keeping to the right-hand side of the

pastures to rejoin the track at the other side of the farm.

At a crossroads of footpaths go straight ahead uphill towards the little gully on the path marked 'Heptonstall Moor and Pennine Way'. The path soon turns up the left side of the little gully ahead.

**❼** As you approach the isolated ruined Clough Head Farm the path dips back into the gully, and goes through a very narrow squeeze stile and gate. As you get near the farmhouse, squeeze through a similar narrow gap in the wall on your left. There is a spring-head by the farm, with built-in stone shelves. Walk past the farm on your left, then follow the path through the gap on the left to continue with the wall on your right and the clough down to your left. Follow the path to the head of the clough.

**❽** At the head of the clough cross the wooden stile between stone walls. Ignore the path that runs left alongside the wall and take the path that veers off slightly to the right of it up onto the moor. This soon joins a peaty track, part of the Pennine Way. Turn left to follow it south south-west over the moor. On a clear day you will see that you are heading straight for Mount Pleasant Farm.

On reaching the farm, the path swings gently to the right and you follow it, with the wall on your left.

**❾** After passing a second farm, Long High Top, the path swings down to the left and continues through a small wooden gate in the left corner. Follow this downhill, between walls for part of the way, through another wooden gate and down

intermittent stone steps until you come out on a lane.

**❿** Turn right for 5 yards along the lane, then turn left down the Pennine Way footpath.

Cross the next road and continue ahead down a farm track, with a small housing estate on your left.

At the end of the track turn left in front of Goose Hey Farm and go through the gate. You are heading for the stile in the far right-hand corner of the field, but you should follow the path close to the wall (ignore the stile ahead in the left corner).

A grassy track between walls takes you down into the valley. After crossing another stile and following another path between fields you enter the wooded, steep-sided Colden Clough itself, with the stream (and, I assume, Wainwright's bridge) 20 yards below you. Turn left to follow the causey-stone path along the left-hand edge of the wood.

**⓫** Continue along the upper boundary of the wood, crossing a stone stile and stepping on some massive boulders that make up the path. Then follow the Calderdale Way (sometimes waymarked with a CW logo in the shape of the clubs symbol on a playing card) across a stone stile out of the wood and across causey stones over the field.

Through the next stile turn right and continue along the causey stones with a wall to your right. Pass through a metal gate and continue along the stones, this time with the wall on your left.

The causey stones run out after you squeeze through by the next gate. After picking your way up over boulders, you should miss out the final section of this walk by continuing up the road and taking the next footpath on the right back to the village. But you will miss some magnificent views…and the climbing is no more demanding than climbing over a sofa.

another squeeze-through with a small wooden gate, you go on to meet a track (marked with a CW logo); turn left and follow it uphill.

⓬ In 70 yards this track joins another at a T-junction. Turn right and in 50 yards take the path along the left side of the stone house. A stone slab stile brings you onto another superb run of stone paving. Such stones 'date back to a time', says Wainwright, 'when there was as much concern for foot-travellers as for those with conveyances'.

The next stile, by a bench, takes you ahead, crossing another footpath, and along to a lane between walls.

In 200 yards, turn left up the narrow road for 100 yards. Then, as the road swings left, take the Calderdale Way into the wood on your right. *Warning*: If you don't have a head for heights and you don't like

⓭ Follow the path, which stays fairly close to the left-hand boundary of the wood. After 60 yards the path goes over boulders. At a marker post follow the Calderdale Way up to the left over a little crag. If you find yourself going downhill and away from the top edge of the wood you have missed this unlikely looking path and you should double back to find it.

⓮ Keep to the path along the top of the ridge with a drystone wall to your left. After walking along the top of the crags, turn left on the footpath between walls through the newer houses of Heptonstall, back into the village.

Aim towards the church. Cross a residential road ahead, turn left on joining a lane and cross another road. Continue through the old town's alleys, keeping the church on your left and take the steps on your left, marked 'Museum, churchyard'; then turn right to return to the main street.

# OXENHOPE

*Length: 4¼ miles*

| Getting there: Oxenhope lies on the A6033, 2 miles south of Haworth. | Parking: The only public parking in the village is on-street. The station car park is for railway users only. | Map: OS Outdoor Leisure 21 South Pennines (GR 032353). |

Take time to explore Oxenhope, spread out along its valley, and you'll find yourself passing abruptly from stone terraced street to rolling pastures. The village had once been what its name suggests, a small enclosed valley (a 'hope'), where oxen were kept. Now it is more celebrated as the end of the line for the Keighley and Worth Valley Railway. It's a perfect period setting for the steam trains which you can see not only close up at the station, but also from a distance, as a cloud of steam puffs up from the valley below. This was originally a branch of the Midland Railway which opened in 1867, helping to transform a weaving and farming village into a small mill town. The mills are now mainly demolished or converted. A large, tree-fringed, mill dam has been replaced by a duck pond at the appropriately named

**FOOD and DRINK**

In Oxenhope there is a choice of pubs which, like the village itself, are spread about. There's a Bay Horse, a Waggon and Horses, and out at the Leeming end of the village the Lamb, where good food is available. There is also a fish and chip shop and village shops. On this walk it is natural to take a break in Haworth, where there are plenty of eating places. We stopped at the first we saw, the Famous Branwell's Tea Rooms (the real Branwell certainly wasn't a famous teetotaller!), down opposite the park, where I enjoyed the home-made vegetable soup, so thick and chunky it was almost piled up in the bowl, a bacon muffin and the chocolate fudge cake.

Mallard View housing development where we saw a dipper on the stream nearby. The village has a park with a play area and sports ground.

Not surprisingly, so near Haworth, the village has Brontë connections. Charlotte tells us that from 1845 to 1849 Patrick Brontë's curate, the Rev Brett Grant, wore out 14 pairs of shoes tramping round to collect donations for the appeal to build the church of St Mary the Virgin in Oxenhope.

No need to wear out any shoes today; this walk follows part of the Worth Way to Haworth and the Brontë Way back to Oxenhope. It is mainly through pastures on the valley slopes, with a short moorland section on Brow Moor. If you find it hard to resist a steam excursion while you're here you could, of course, do one half of the walk then return by train.

THE WALK

❶ With the station car park behind you, turn left along Mill Lane which leads off Station Road, crossing Bridgehouse Beck. After 100 yards, cross the main road ahead and walk up Dark Lane opposite.

❷ In 400 yards turn left along a narrow path behind the garden of the stone farmhouse at Little Haley. After a stile and a squeeze-through wall opening, follow the path through a metal gate behind Lower Haley Farm. A second gate ahead takes you along a green lane between stone walls.

❸ After 150 yards at the end of the lane, cross the step stile, then head at an angle of 45 degrees to the far right-hand corner of the field. Take the squeeze stile into the next field and again head for the far right corner, keeping close to the wall on your right.

This next stile brings you out on a lane. Follow the lane to the right, up the hill, ignoring the gated track immediately to your right.

❹ After passing the farmhouse at the end of the lane, take a short, grassy track between two walls up the hill. Cross the stile by the gate and turn left, to cross a small field, following a tumbling old wall on your left.

Take the next stile by a gate and cross rough pasture. After crossing the line of a broken wall, take the lower track ahead, which will bring you out on a lane.

❺ Turn left (signed 'Worth Way, Hebden Road'), then, after a small turning circle to Delf Hill Farm, take the metal gate to the grassy track ahead. Just before the track turns down to a farmhouse take the public footpath through a narrow wooden gate. This takes you along a grassy slope immediately above the farm.

❻ A narrow gate brings you out on the access road to the farm. Cross it, follow a

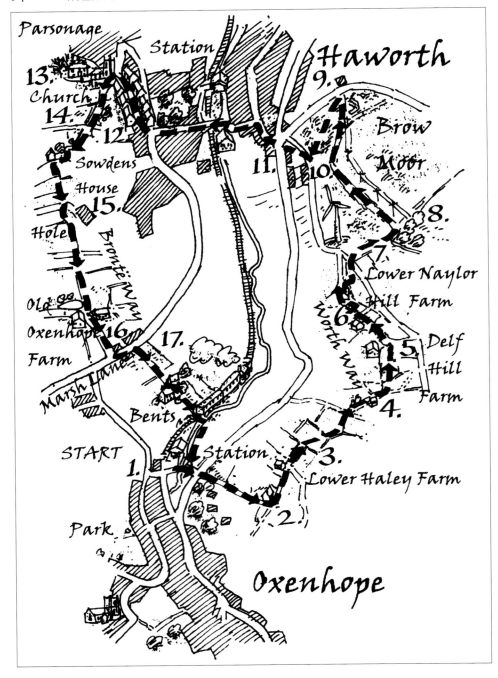

wall of massive stones on your right for 50 yards, then go through a tiny stile to a small grassy slope.

At the top of the slope, turn left and walk to the far side of Lower Naylor Hill Farm, keeping the buildings on your right. Immediately after the buildings take the nine concrete steps on your right to climb a stile in the wall, then turn left along the edge of the moor.

❼ At the road turn left and, after 50 yards, turn right along the Worth Way up onto Brow Moor. After 200 yards you reach a shelter belt of trees behind the high wall on your right. In a further 100 yards opposite a metal gate in the wall, take the peaty track on your left, where the 'Bleak House spur' power line heads out across the moor.

❽ In 400 yards the track swings to the right and in another 200 yards, just before you get to a power-line pole on the right of the track, take the small path winding to the left through the heather.

❾ At the quarry, before you reach the bend in the road, take a sharp left turn onto another heathery track.

❿ When you come to the road by some cottages, turn right and take a steep footpath down the left-hand side of the triangle of rough ground. This brings you out at a small turning circle on Brow Top Road.

⓫ Turn left, cross Hebden Road and continue down steeply sloping Brow Road.

*Oxenhope station.*

When you come out on Station Road turn left (*or right to take the train back to Oxenhope*) over the bridge and continue up the hill, passing a park on your right.

**⓬** Cross the road to take the cobbled street up to Haworth church and parsonage.

**⓭** Walk through the gates in front of the church and turn left to find the Brontë Way. A kissing-gate takes you out of the churchyard, then along a paved footpath.

**⓮** Continue along on the footpath signposted 'Brontë Way to Hole ¼ mile Oxenhope 1½ miles', ignoring the footpath to 'Top Withens and Brontë Falls' to the right. The walled footpath zigzags around Sowdens House. After crossing a stile, turn

left and follow the wall on the left-hand side of the pastures.

**⓯** When a squeeze stile by an iron gate brings you out on a lane, turn right and immediately left alongside the wall at the top of the slope on the path marked 'Brontë Way to Oxenhope'. Follow the Brontë Way straight ahead for the next ¼ mile, keeping close to the left-hand side of the next three fields; but in the fourth, as you near Old Oxenhope Farm, with a large pond beside it, you should have the wall on your right.

**⓰** A stile by the farm gate takes you out onto Old Oxenhope Lane. Turn left and, in 200 yards at the T-junction with Marsh Lane, turn left again.

**⓱** In 100 yards turn right on a footpath which follows a farm track. It turns left in front of Bents House (which featured in the film *The Railway Children*), then immediately right and through a stile down towards the railway. As the sign says, 'Beware of trains' as you use the crossing. Cross the metal footbridge over Bridgehouse Beck and turn immediately right to follow the beckside path back to Mill Lane and the start of the walk.